FINDING YOUR AUTISTIC SUPERPOWER

Christine Lion

Copyright © 2020 Christine Lion

All rights reserved.

This book is dedicated to all the neurodiverse women I've met in my life who have made my world a bit less lonely and a lot more interesting.

CONTENTS

Introduction 1
What is autism? 10
Social interaction 30
Changes and details 57
Sensory sensitivity 72
Stimming 101
Executive functioning 107
Special interests 122
Controlling your emotions 129
Taking care of your health 149
School 171
Work 194
Sex and relationships 204
Being abused 221
Getting diagnosed 236
Superpowers 248

Introduction

Why I have written this book

"If he goes over to another boy and hits him, he won't understand why the other boy gets upset," said one of the parents on my swim team when I was young. "But why?" I asked, still not understanding what she was trying to tell me. "He's autistic, so he doesn't have normal feelings or empathy like us," she continued, probably already annoyed with my questions.

So that's what I grew up thinking autism was. Some sort of "disease" that could take people's feelings away and make them unable to communicate with the world around them. And it never crossed my mind that it could happen to anyone other than boys.

At the same time, I knew I didn't fit into the world I lived in. I felt like there was no way for me to properly reach other people. No matter what I said or did, it wasn't understood by others. They would think I was mean, rude or just weird. There was a handbook to life that someone had forgotten to give me, and I would pass out from exhaustion after trying manoeuvre the world without it.

Every year when I left school during the summer holidays, I dreamt about returning in the fall, completely transformed. This would make everyone like me and want to become friends with me. I also had desperate fantasies about taking over someone else's body. Anyone's. Because it had to be better than being trapped in my mind all alone.

After starting university, I slowly found a tribe of friends. They were all a bit different from the rest of the people I studied with. Opinionated and not afraid of stepping over social boundaries. When we sat down in the school cafeteria, we had a standing joke that people around us would leave because they got so uncomfortable from listening to our conversations.

But I still couldn't pinpoint what exactly made me stand out from other people in general. And I don't know what made me start looking into Asperger's and autism. It could have been comments from others. More than one person has joked that I remind them of Sheldon in the Big Bang Theory. Some people have even used Asperger's as an insult towards me long before I considered that I might be on the spectrum.

I started taking online tests for Asperger's and autism in my early twenties. Just for fun, I thought to myself. My score was high. Far above the threshold for being considered for a diagnosis. I didn't take it too seriously, and I told myself the classic line that all autistic people hate; "everyone is on the spectrum." And I thought that if I just tried a little harder to be normal, I would finally be one of those girls that jumped effortlessly from conversation to conversation, and I would stop feeling like I didn't belong.

But that wasn't the case. I never "got better." I just spent most of my energy and willpower trying to pass as a neurotypical person. And believe me, that takes a lot of effort. Which is why women on the spectrum often end up completely burnt out if they go undiagnosed for too long. They crash both mentally and physically because they work so hard to hide the things that make them seem different.

When I finally decided to look into autism properly, it was eye-opening. There was so much more to it than I had thought. Yes, trouble with social situations is a big part of it, but almost as important are other things like dependency on routines, reluctance to change, sensory overload and meltdowns. So many of the issues I had struggled with my entire life.

And I had thought the reason I was troubled was that I wasn't trying hard enough. That I was failing. This new understanding suddenly gave me the tools to understand and accept myself on a whole new level. It explained the mechanisms I was using to cope in everyday life, and it also gave me ideas to improve in the areas where I struggled.

But what I also realised, was that autism wasn't only an explanation for negative things that had happened in my life. It could also explain several of my positive traits and why I seemed to excel so naturally in some areas.

There are so many misconceptions about autism. That all it does is ruin lives and tear families apart. That it's an evil infection that takes over your body. But autism isn't just one thing, and it's not just negative. Of course there will be tough times, and some things are hard. But autism doesn't mean broken.

Autism isn't just a diagnosis. It's a part of who you are. Would I have changed it if I had the chance? If you asked me when I was ten years old, I would have said yes without hesitation. But if you ask me today, with the knowledge of what autism is, I wouldn't give it up.

I think there are several things we need to work on because we're challenged by a world where the majority of the population are neurotypicals, and I acknowledge that we'll probably meet a lot of obstacles in our lives. But there are ways of improving and working with what we have.

There are also ways of celebrating the gifts that come with our way of thinking. I believe most people on the spectrum have some kind of superpower. But it doesn't mean I believe everyone with autism is Rain Man, and that's a myth that hurts us more than it helps.

You can then criticise me for writing a book about autistic superpowers in the first place since this only enforces the misconception about autistic people as human calculators. But I'm not saying that we're all as a group better than neurotypicals. And more importantly, I'm not saying that we're worse either. We're complex and different, and we're not a stereotype. But since so much of the media's focus is about our weaknesses, I wanted to write something realistic that also captures our strengths.

With autistic people's unique perspective comes so many opportunities to do things in a new way. I want us to celebrate those differences, and I want to help you discover your strengths.

I chose to write this book so that other women on the spectrum, if they're diagnosed or not, can have the tools to understand themselves. This is the book I always wanted to read when I was going through my diagnostic process but couldn't find.

And it doesn't really matter if the person reading this book isn't a woman, or doesn't qualify for a full autism diagnosis. If you struggle with some of the same issues as autism is known for, you can benefit from exploring those further.

I want you to use this book as a way to get to know yourself. Take my experiences and use them as your own. Build your image around what you can do and how you want to live your life. Not around other people's limitations.

Who am I to speak on behalf of everyone with autism? No one. Because even if I'm on the spectrum, I don't think that I can properly understand how every other autistic person is feeling. We're all so different, and we all have our own struggles. That I'm able to do something, doesn't mean that someone else can do exactly the same.

And you can easily criticise me for writing a book about how wonderful autism can be sometimes. I have a good job, friends and I'm married to someone I love. Life must have come easy for me. But trust me when I say that it didn't, and it still doesn't. I work hard on many of the things I mention in this book, but I also try to celebrate the good things autism has given me, and I want to share that with others so they can feel the same way.

How the book is structured

Each of the chapters in this book is dedicated to areas where people on the spectrum are different from neurotypicals. Some chapters will naturally focus more on things we struggle with, while others will cover our strengths.

In each chapter, I'll try to give a balanced view based on both research and my own experiences. I often think that books where the authors don't spend any time backing up the things they say with research are missing the point. And you'll see that in addition to quoting results from studies, I also go through the research methods where this can be relevant for the results.

But I don't think that research and numbers are the only things that matter. I also believe it adds value to read about someone else's personal experiences. It can give you a sense of belonging when you for the first time see that there are people just like you who are going through the same. And when I first started reading books by other autistic women, I loved to read their personal examples. Finally, I wasn't alone, and I could see myself in someone else. Which is why I've chosen to be quite personal in this book.

In addition to our superpowers, I'll talk about things autistic people typically struggle with, and I'll give you examples and tips that I've found helpful myself.

When I give tips and pointers, I'm not doing it because I think you should change who you are by trying to come across as neurotypical. I don't want you to suppress what makes you special. That's exactly what I tried to do the first part of my life and I don't recommend it. But knowing where you have weaknesses or where others could misunderstand you will give you a better starting point to decide how you want to live your life.

At the end of each chapter, I've added useful tasks for you to work on. It will help you decide if there are things you want to change, but it will also help you map out your strengths and what to do with them. But as with many things in life, you only need to do them if and when you find them helpful.

On my website, christinelion.com, I have uploaded pdfs with worksheets for most of the chapters as well. They don't contain any more information than you can find in the book, but if you want space to write and fill things out, downloading these will be easier.

Writing style

There are many opinions about how we should properly

describe people on the spectrum. One of the core conflicts is if it's correct to use "people-first" or "identity-first" language. I got pretty confused the first time I heard about this because I didn't understand the concept. But since I know that language is powerful, I tried to understand what the opposing sides thought.

Those who support the "people-first" way of speaking claim that it's only correct to say "person with autism," because autism shouldn't define who you are. It seems like this argumentation is mostly coming from parents with autistic kids, and not so much from autistic people themselves.

If you support "identity-first" language, you say or write "autistic person," because autism is such a core part of who you are. It's not a disease. It's not a temporary state and it won't pass like the flu. It's a neurodivergent difference in the way our brains work and as much a part of us as our skin colour or our age.

In most support groups for autistic people, you'll find that there's a preference to be described as autistic instead of "having" autism. I think this should be respected, and I find it disturbing that some people who aren't autistic will try to control how we talk about ourselves. Even the spelling software I used when writing this book tried to autocorrect me when I wrote "autistic person" and said it was offensive. It wanted me to change it to "person with autism," which I didn't feel the need to do.

Then there are those who prefer to think of themselves as having Asperger's. This used to be a diagnosis that was separate from autism, but it has now been included in the broader term Autism Spectrum Disorder (ASD), which is why I'll use autism throughout this book and not Asperger's.

Some people, like me, also refer to themselves as "on the spectrum" or "on the autism spectrum." There are tons of other nicknames and abbreviations people like to use, and I think it's perfectly fine for anyone to say what they like as long as they don't try to control what an autistic person chooses to use.

I've found that there isn't one correct way to describe an autistic person, but I respect that there are differences. Since I'm on the spectrum myself, I feel like I have a bit more creative freedom than if I wasn't, and sometimes I'll say that I have autism without meaning anything further by it.

If you're on the spectrum or not, I ask you not to take it as an insult. Since I'm autistic, I tend to hurt other people's feelings unintentionally quite often. So please try to remember just that.

You'll also see that I talk about neurotypicals frequently throughout this book. That's the word for someone who isn't on the autism spectrum. I don't want to refer to them as "normal" people, as they're not the standard that we're comparing ourselves against.

Another thing I'll avoid in most of the book is referring to people as "high-functioning" or "low-functioning." It's used by many, including medical professionals, to describe how much help someone on the spectrum needs. They will often refer to someone as high-functioning if they have a normal or high IQ, but I'll discuss in a later chapter why this way of categorising us isn't very helpful. You'll also not see me talking about "severe" autism anywhere for the same reasons – it's wildly inaccurate and invalidating.

Because I know that many of the people reading this book will struggle with traumatic or uncomfortable experiences from their own lives, I'll try to add a trigger warning where I believe this is needed. For most chapters though, you'll be able to guess what it contains, so feel free to skip those you don't want to read or come back later when you think you're in a better place to read and process it.

And before you go ahead with the rest, I would like to

apologise for my sometimes weak word choices. After living two years in England, my English is unfortunately not yet good enough to make everything float as it should, but I'm too much of a control freak to let anyone else translate for me.

What is autism?

Where the autism diagnosis comes from

Even though several studies indicate that autism has a genetic link, there is no blood test you can take to tell if you're autistic (Abrahams & Geschwind, 2008; Krumm et al., 2013). This means that a diagnosis is made on the basis of conversations and observations. And the person getting diagnosed will be judged after clinical diagnostic criteria. To make it even more difficult, there isn't just one set of criteria to get a diagnosis.

There are two main sets of standards to diagnose psychiatric diseases and disabilities (autism is currently defined as a disability). The DSM-5 criteria are set by the American Psychiatric Association, and the ICD-11 criteria are set by the World Health Organisation. These standards are also updated from time to time. This is indicated by the number at the end, meaning the DSM-5 came after the DSM-4.

The last significant revision of the criteria for autism came from the launch of the DSM-5 in 2013. One of the major changes was that Asperger's syndrome was removed as a separate diagnosis.

In some countries, Asperger's is still used, and many people on the spectrum who received this diagnosis originally will still prefer to say that they have Asperger's instead of autism. Also, since many people aren't aware of the removal of Asperger's, you might need to explain that what they used to think of as Asperger's is now a part of Autism Spectrum Disorder.

Even though the diagnostic criteria and name have been updated several times throughout the years, autism has always existed. It was first described by Leo Kanner in 1943. He studied children who were brought to him by their parents because of their "strange" behaviour. Most of them were non-verbal, had a strong need for routines, and showed little to no interest in other people. Instead of labelling the children as schizophrenic, which was normal at the time, Kanner started using the term "infantile autism."

In 1944, Hans Asperger was working with a group of children with similar characteristics. But these kids could keep long one-sided conversations, had intense special interests and were described as highly intellectual. Asperger said that they had "autistic psychopathy." It wasn't until Lorna Wing wrote about his research in the 80s that the term Asperger's syndrome was used, and as mentioned above, it was taken away again in 2013.

Although there are genes linked to autism, there's no single explanation for what causes someone to become autistic. There's also no simple explanation for why autistic people are different from neurotypicals. But there have been several attempts at finding one single cause for all the symptoms.

One of the explanations says that autistic people lack "theory of mind," meaning that we can't understand what other people think or feel, or put ourselves in their place. If this was correct, it could explain some of our difficulties socialising, but it doesn't explain the other ranges of symptoms like sensory sensitivity or the need for stimming.

Others think autism is caused by having an "extreme male brain." Simon Baron-Cohen, who is a well-known autism researcher, tried to explain that people on the spectrum are a product of having too strong male qualities. And indeed, there *is* some research suggesting that increased levels of androgens could affect genes that are related to the risk of autism (Quartier et al., 2018), as well as some descriptions saying that girls with autism act more like "tomboys" (Knickmeyer et al., 2007).

But looking deeper into this, what is femininity exactly? Is it all the ridiculous standards of beauty and behaviour that we teach girls are the only appropriate options for them? To sit still, put on an uncomfortable dress, entertain strangers who want to talk to us, not smudge the lipstick and act grateful when a man gives us attention? These are all impossible social standards that make no sense. And since the autistic mind doesn't like to follow arbitrary rules without reason, of course women and girls on the spectrum tend to avoid those things.

But Baron-Cohen's theory isn't based on how feminine autistic women act. It's based on something he named the "empathising-systemising theory." It gives men and women two opposing skills and says that they can have one or the other. Either, you're good at "systemising" or you're good at empathy.

But who says you have to have poor empathy if you're good at systemising and vice versa? I find it hard to believe that all our capabilities and strengths can be placed on a linear scale from least to most, and that being good at one thing takes away from the other.

I also don't think that the division of men and women into two categories where men are good at building systems and women are good at empathy, are easy to study. It introduces so many cultural biases that it would be impossible to prove.

A theory I find more believable is that sensory issues can be behind many of the typical autistic traits. When we're constantly overwhelmed by information our senses need to interpret, it's difficult to control how we socialise with others. But I also don't think that this theory offers a complete explanation of what makes us different from neurotypicals.

Some theories have bits and pieces that I feel fit with how I experience the world, while others seem like they're far fetched. What's definitely true is that autism isn't caused by vaccines, cellphones or whatever else is the latest conspiracy theory.

Autism is a life-long difference in how our brain works, and this causes individuals on the spectrum to both act differently and experience the world in a different manner than others.

So where does autism end and where do you begin? What parts of you come from autism and what are just different styles of personality? I don't think there's a definite answer to that. Autism is a part of you, and it always will be. You can change how you react in certain situations, but you can't change who you are.

Curing autism isn't possible, and if it was, it would turn you into a completely different person. Autism isn't a "layer" that's added on top of a neurotypical person, it's a completely different set of abilities and challenges that make you unique.

How many people are autistic?

You've probably heard people talking about the "autism epidemic" while referring to the fact that more and more people seem to get an autism diagnosis. But what gives them that impression?

In the US, the ADDM network (Autism and Developmental Disabilities Monitoring) estimate the prevalence of autism in 8-year old children. They have done this using a similar research method every few years since 2000, which means they have been able to identify trends in the population. In the year 2000, only 1 in 150 children was estimated to be on the spectrum, while in 2014 as many as 1 in 68 met the criteria (Baio et al., 2018). Does this mean that there has been an explosion in people being born with autistic traits? Not necessarily.

Since the ADDM network only goes through observations that have been noted in school or health records, the numbers are better at describing the trend of how many people with autism get picked up by different support systems. This means that the trend might not actually come from an increase in the number of autistic children, but an increase in how many are described as having traits that fit with the autism criteria. It can mean people get better at recognising children who need support.

Historically, children have more often been diagnosed with autism if they have learning disabilities or if they score poorly on intelligence tests. But as we become better and better at identifying symptoms of autism, kids with normal or high IQs are also getting diagnosed.

And this is exactly what the ADDM-studies are showing us. More and more children with autism fall within the range of what is called normal to high IQs. From 2000 to 2014, the percentage of autistic children who also had an IQ that fell within the range of intellectual disabilities fell from roughly half to one third (Baio et al., 2018).

In the ADDM study from 2014, there were four boys with autism identified for every girl, which is a pretty big difference, but much less than what has been seen in other studies, and especially when compared with numbers for adults.

I think that one of the reasons for this is that girls with normal and high IQs have been more frequently overlooked than boys. And this is also supported by the data. The percentage of girls with low IQs fell from 60 to 35% between 2000 and 2014, while the trend for boys showed a decline from 40 to 30% in the same period.

Studies that have looked at how frequent autism is in adults are also estimating that there are a lot fewer autistic women than men. According to the Adult Psychiatric Morbidity Survey from 2007, only 0.2% of adult women in the UK are autistic. While the same study estimates that 1.8% of men in the UK are on the spectrum (Bebbington et al., 2009).

To understand the numbers and how much one should trust them, I like to look into the methods used. The quality of the study is good, and they have randomly selected people to participate in screenings and assessments, which means it avoids some of the issues with self-selection, and it will also make sure that it picks up people showing traits of autism even though they might not have a previous diagnosis.

However, as with all research, there are some weaknesses. First of all, quite a lot of the people who were asked to participate in the study dropped out, but we don't know if this skewed the numbers for women in any way.

Of the people with a high score on the screening test, only a few were selected to have an actual assessment. The assessments were done through interviews by people who had clinical training, but they weren't specialists with experience in assessing women. And it has been indicated that women are severely under-diagnosed if they're assessed by someone without experience, which I'll come back to later in this chapter. Therefore, I have some doubts that the level of autism amongst adult women is really as low as 0.2%.

Another study that indicates that these estimates are likely to be wrong looked at 3-year olds in a high-risk group. Here, researchers found that 19.6% of the girls and 32.4% of the boys were autistic (Zwaigenbaum et al., 2012). These numbers are of course high because the children were picked from a group with high probability of autism, but the interesting part is to look at the relationship between diagnosed girls and boys. 1.65 boys were diagnosed for every girl, which is quite different from the relationship of 9 men to every woman found in the UK study above.

So more and more people are getting diagnosed as autistic, but that doesn't mean autism is becoming more common now than it was before. In fact, I think many people, especially women, still remain undiagnosed.

But with more people getting diagnosed than before, is there any truth to the statement that "we're all a little autistic"? Several people who aren't defined as autistic might share some of our issues. For example can you have sensory sensitivity without being on the autism spectrum.

The problem with stating that you're "a bit autistic" is that you're invalidating the struggles of someone with autism. It doesn't mean that I think people shouldn't be allowed to have the same kind of support or resources for their issues, but I hope they consider how it makes an autistic person feel if they say that everyone is autistic in some way.

I also realise that for some people, saying that everyone has autistic traits is their way of saying they think they're on the spectrum too. It can be a way of dipping their toe into the water to see how it feels. Maybe they suspect that they're on the spectrum, but are afraid to look into it.

With more knowledge and awareness of autism spreading, I hope that we can all become more tolerant of each other's needs and respect that neurodiversity is here to stay. And with that, more people are likely going to be open about their autism diagnosis, and we can have an honest and open dialogue about how to help each other.

How autism is different for women

In general, the main symptoms of autism that are described in the DSM-5 and ICD-11 are difficulty in social interactions, trouble with change, limited range of interests, sensory sensitivity and in some cases also clumsiness and trouble with speech. It's also necessary for the symptoms to be present your entire life, as autism is a lifelong disorder and not something you acquire as you get older.

The criteria are updated to reflect current research, but most of the studies done on autism are based on men or boys. This means that the criteria used to make a diagnosis don't take into account that the symptoms can be different for women. And as a result, many women and girls are either misdiagnosed or not diagnosed at all (Kirkovski et al., 2013).

Women are in general better at imaginative play, have different special interests than most boys, and can be very good at learning social skills. But in addition, women score lower on executive functioning and can have more difficulty with friendships (Kirkovski et al., 2013).

One study looked at boys and girls who either came in just below or above the threshold for receiving an official autism diagnosis. Many of the girls scored very high on traits for autism but still didn't meet the criteria for getting diagnosed. And the girls who did end up with a diagnosis had a lot more additional problems like low IQs or behavioural difficulties. The same pattern wasn't found for boys (Dworzynski et al., 2012).

This is further backed up by the study from the ADDM which showed that more of the autistic girls had low IQs or learning disabilities. Research also shows that autistic girls with high IQ are less likely to meet the criteria for some types of diagnostic interviews like the ADI-R (Ratto et al., 2018).

And even when boys and girls have the same level of symptoms indicating that they're autistic, the boys are much more likely to receive a diagnosis (Russel et al., 2010). This can mean that the women and girls who are getting diagnosed are struggling more than the average autistic boy or man.

Autistic girls are also less likely to be discovered and diagnosed early. In fact, a Dutch study confirmed that girls with Asperger's syndrome were diagnosed on average two years later than boys (Begeer et al., 2013). While teachers or parents often react when little boys aren't playing like the other kids or have an intense interest in trains or car brands, the autistic girls fly under the radar.

For example, most adults wouldn't think twice if they saw a girl playing with barbie dolls. I loved my dolls as a kid, but I didn't like the idea of playing with them as much as collecting sets of them. It's not the typical play you might expect from a girl, but since it looks so similar to what a neurotypical girl would do, no one thinks what we're doing is a sign of autism.

Women are also known for being good to "mask" their symptoms by learning how to consciously change their behaviour and mimic others. Some even mask their symptoms so well that they're never diagnosed, or they're diagnosed very late in life. This is especially the case for women without any types of learning disabilities. They often use some of their intellectual capacity to analyse social situations and make conscious decisions to act in a certain way that's more "socially acceptable."

These women will often not be discovered until they're so

exhausted from all this extra work that they collapse. This has a name, and it's called "autistic burnout." But even when women seek help for this, they're more likely to be diagnosed with something else. Popularly, women are diagnosed with eating disorders, depression, social anxiety or bipolar personality disorder because so many professionals fail to recognise that autism is the cause of their symptoms.

And even if women discover autism for themselves and actively seek out a doctor to get diagnosed, many end up being ignored because they don't fit the typical male profile.

A UK qualitative study sought to find out how the female autism differs from the male by doing in-depth interviews with women who were diagnosed as adults. It found several common themes amongst the participants. One was that they often had their concerns dismissed or ignored by their primary doctors when they asked to be assessed for autism. One woman in the study had even been told she was "too poor at maths to be autistic." And many of them had been misdiagnosed and treated for depression or anxiety without autism ever being mentioned as a reason for their problems (Bargiela, 2016).

In another qualitative study where researchers interviewed girls on the spectrum and their mothers, the process of getting a diagnosis was described as very challenging. And most of the mothers said it seemed like it was a much harder process for them than it had been for boys in their communities (Cridland et al., 2014).

It seems like the reason women are being ignored isn't just that the diagnostic criteria don't fully reflect the female presentation of autism, but also that medical personnel don't take women and girls seriously when they ask for an assessment.

The big myth

There are many misconceptions and myths about people on the spectrum. Often because of the way autistic people are portrayed in the media. We're either stupid, emotionless and incapable of taking care of ourselves, or we're weird geniuses who fail in all other areas of life.

On average, autistic people have more extreme traits than neurotypicals, but it doesn't mean people on the spectrum are incapable of doing great things. Some of us are non-verbal, struggle with learning disabilities and need extra support. But we can also create amazing things within our area of expertise because we're able to see the world in a whole new way.

Historically, autism has been associated with lower than average IQ. But people with lower IQs and learning disabilities are often easier to identify because they more frequently need help. And people with high IQs frequently mask their symptoms or use their intelligence to cover up weaknesses in areas of their lives where they struggle. This means there's likely a greater portion of autistic people with high or normal IQs who are undiagnosed, and the averages we see in research are skewed.

From the US study of 8-year olds, there was a clear trend showing that of the autistic children, less and less of them each year were classified as having an IQ lower than 70. And when we know that more and more people are diagnosed, I believe we're better able to identify those with high intelligence who have previously been overlooked.

And I'm one of those people. In my early twenties, I decided to take an IQ test arranged by Mensa because I didn't fit in anywhere and it seemed like all my achievements were purely academic. It turned out I scored amongst the top 2% and was offered a membership there.

This sounds like great news, but I always thought of it as a double-edged sword. While I did great in school and learnt new things very easily, it made me seem even more different from the other kids I wanted to socialise with. The high intelligence also made me seem too "smart and successful" for anyone to consider that I was autistic. Which means that it took me a long time to realise that I wasn't a misfit or a freak.

I could have saved myself a lot of self-hatred and trouble if I had known I was on the spectrum. There are so many times I should have forgiven myself instead of thinking I was stupid or unlikeable. And that's also the case for many other women on the spectrum who live most of their lives without knowing they have autism. It's about time researchers, doctors and therapists realise that smart and successful women can be autistic too. And hopefully, that will happen sooner later than later.

Some researchers have even considered that genes correlated with autism are also found in people with higher than average intelligence. Evolutionary biology professor Bernard Crespi published a theory in 2016 that said autism is associated with risk factors for having high intelligence. In fact, he calls it "enhanced, but unbalanced components of intelligence" (Crespi, 2016). Meaning we can severely outperform neurotypicals in some areas, but at the same time struggle in others.

And he's not the only one who has been looking at autism as a disorder of high intelligence. Using data from the UK Biobank, researchers have discovered that having a genetically increased risk for autism is associated with higher levels of education and better performance on cognitive tests. This doesn't mean that all the individuals included in the test have autism, only that their genetical makeup show an increased risk (Hagenaars, 2016).

When researching relatives of autistic people, Simon Baron-Cohen and his colleagues looked at students at Cambridge who were studying Literature, Physics, Engineering or Mathematics.

It turned out that the people studying the three latter subjects had more autistic relatives (Baron-Cohen et al., 1998).

It doesn't necessarily indicate that people with autistic relatives are smarter, as Literature students at Cambridge are certainly very clever. But I dare to say that there's a specific type of intelligence and interest amongst people who do well in Physics or Mathematics.

But these studies are still all about genetical risk factors and relatives of autistic people, and not so much about autistic people's performances. However, there are also several interesting observations in which autistic people outperform neurotypicals.

Children with autism are for example better at finding causal relationships. Kids with and without autism were tested for their drive to find explanations in situations with both technical and social problems. In the first test, they were asked to balance a block that was impossible to balance. The autistic kids showed a stronger interest in inspecting the block to try to figure out why it didn't work as expected. However, in the social experiment, where they were supposed to explore why a researcher stopped handing them stickers, the autistic children showed less interest than the neurotypicals (Rutherford and Subiaul, 2015).

This is an interesting observation that says something about our abilities and interests, and it can explain why so many autistic people excel at typical difficult topics like Mathematics, Physics and Engineering that are driven by finding logical explanations.

However, many are tired of the stereotypical Rain Man representation of autism. Someone with a disability showing superior skills in one area like this are often called Savants. But the truth is that savant skills are more common amongst autistic people than you might think (Meilleur et al., 2014; Howlin et al.,

2009).

Typical areas of excellence are art, music, mathematics, memory and spatial skills. It has for example been shown that a subgroup of people on the spectrum has enhanced auditory processing and better memory for melodies (Jones et al., 2009; Stanutz et al., 2014). When quantitative studies have been done, not all people on the spectrum show these types of abilities, but it has been clearly demonstrated that our uneven skillset not only means we perform poorly in some areas; we also sometimes outperform our neurotypical peers.

But it doesn't mean that our abilities to do well in those areas make us completely unable to do other things. Autistic people are capable of forming friendships and feeling love. And if we're not all great at calculating square roots in our head, it doesn't mean we can't have other special interests or skills that are highly valuable.

Self-work

If you're not sure if you have autistic traits or not, there are many tests you can take on your own before talking to a doctor or therapist. There are several tests available online to screen for autism symptoms, and if you want to take one of them, you should search for "the autism spectrum quotient."

But this test is modelled from mostly male responses, so I've tried to gather some questions that are specific for autistic women. They're based on my own experiences, research for this book, as well as discussions with other women on the spectrum.

The more times you answer "yes" on the questions below, the more autistic traits you have. But remember that this isn't an "official" test, and it's also normal for someone who isn't on the spectrum to recognise themselves in several of the traits below.

Autistic traits:

1. Have you always felt like you don't fit in with your peers?
2. Did you tend to spend time with either much older or much younger kids when you were young, or even with adults only?
3. Do you prefer socialising with only one person instead of in a big group?
4. Are you exhausted after a day surrounded by other people and need to spend time alone to recuperate?
5. Do you change the way you speak according to the person you're talking to, for example by mimicking dialect or posture?
6. Do people often feel offended by something you said, or do they consider something you said to be rude?
7. Have you spent time reading about socialising and body language?
8. Do you often realise after you have said something that the other person might have misunderstood you?
9. Do you replay conversations in your head either before or after they happen?
10. Do you feel like you have no or very few close friends?
11. Were you ever bullied or teased when you were younger?
12. Do you dislike asking for help at school, work or in your personal life?
13. Do you feel like you're only able to socialise with a drink in your hand?
14. Do you pay more attention to things than to people?
15. Do you often want to leave a social setting to do something else?
16. Do other people think you're weird or eccentric?
17. Do you hate conflicts but still tend to get angry at

people?
18. Do you feel like you need to fake it all the time to fit in socially?
19. Do you have one or several very strong interests (they might change frequently or stay the same all the time)?
20. Do you collect things?
21. Do you hate small talk?
22. Do you think other people's conversations are boring but light up if you can talk about a topic you're interested in?
23. Do you often not understand when people get bored by talking to you?
24. Are you upset if plans are cancelled or changed at short notice?
25. Do you eat a certain type of food each day for breakfast or other meals for months or years at a time?
26. Do you like having the same routine every day?
27. Do you get upset if something you had planned on eating is no longer available?
28. Have you had eating disorders?
29. Are you very stretchy or hypermobile?
30. Have you been diagnosed with PTSD, depression, BPD, ADHD or other psychological disorders?
31. Do you have problems with your digestion or have you been diagnosed with IBS?
32. Do you have a strong sense of justice?
33. Do you hate compromises because you think something is either right or wrong?
34. Do you hate it when people tell lies, even if it's white lies?
35. Are you too honest?
36. Do you often interpret things literally?
37. Do you either not understand or not like other people's jokes or sarcasm?

38. Do you get along much better with people who are on the spectrum than with neurotypicals?
39. Do you often feel like you get misunderstood in conversations?
40. Do you feel uncomfortable talking on the phone?
41. Do you often interrupt other people or struggle to know when it's your turn to talk?
42. Do you go quiet in big group settings but don't notice until later because you're busy trying to process all the different conversations happening at once?
43. Are you bad at aerobics classes or following instructions?
44. Do you talk either too loudly or too softly?
45. Do you spill food when you eat or drop things on the floor?
46. Do you often get bruises because you bump into things?
47. Were you bad at playing ball games when you were a kid?
48. Are you bad at multitasking?
49. Do you hate certain types of clothes that don't fit in a specific way (too loose, too tight, itchy)?
50. Do you avoid certain types of fabrics and cut off labels inside your clothes?
51. Are you often overwhelmed by too much noise around you?
52. Do you have trouble sorting out the voices on a television show?
53. Are you easily distracted by things going on in the background?
54. Do you hear sounds other people don't hear or are annoyed by sounds others have no problems with?
55. Are you easily moved by music, books or films (for example get goosebumps when you listen to music you like)?

56. Do you wear headphones whenever you're outside?
57. Do other people comment that you look sad or angry when you're happy?
58. Do you fidget with your hair, nails, pens, or other things around you?
59. Do you frequently go on social media instead of paying attention during a conversation?
60. Do you tend to bite your lips, inside your cheeks, on pens, your nails or other things?
61. Do you hate certain types of food because of the way they taste or smell?
62. Are you repulsed by some types of smells but love others?
63. Do you tap your fingers or move your legs all the time?
64. Do you dislike getting wet?
65. Do you hate wearing makeup or having anything on your face?
66. Do you enjoy strong pressure or using a weighted blanket when you sleep?
67. Do you feel closer to animals than to people?
68. Are you either very emotional or not showing feelings at all?
69. Are you very visual and have artistic talent?
70. Are you very good with numbers, patterns and logic?
71. Do you either commit to things fully or not at all?
72. Do you often miss paying bills on time or not open mail or emails?
73. Do you avoid picking up the phone if someone calls you unexpectedly or not open the door if someone rings the doorbell?
74. Are you often late for appointments or forget things?
75. Do you frequently lose things like cellphone, keys or misplace smaller items?

76. Do you sometimes forget to shower for days or wash your hair because you're too busy or distracted?
77. Do you have trouble respecting authorities?
78. Have you ever been sexually abused?
79. Have you been in an abusive relationship?
80. Do you have difficulties knowing where your boundaries are?
81. When you date someone, can you get intense very early in the relationship?
82. Do you have an uneven profile of abilities?
83. Do you have a high IQ or are considered very smart by friends?
84. Do you have a very good long-term memory, but can forget things you just heard or saw?
85. Do you often get caught in a spiral of negative thinking for days at a time?
86. Do you have trouble finding your way inside large buildings, for example at a university or a train station?
87. Did you drop out of classes at university?
88. Do you have trouble keeping a job, or do you prefer to work for yourself where you can be in charge of what you do?
89. Do you hate going to long meetings?
90. Do you often get overwhelmed or stressed if you get too many tasks at once and end up avoiding them all instead of prioritising?
91. Do you strive for perfection even if it's not essential for the bigger picture?
92. Are you very attentive to details, for example by finding four-leaf clovers?
93. Have you often been taken advantage of by friends or partners asking you to sacrifice a lot without getting anything in return?

94. Is it hard for you to identify precisely what you're feeling?
95. Are you seen as very serious by others?
96. Do you point it out if other people misspell something or make a mistake?
97. Do you hate changes in your environment?
98. Do you get angry if other people move your stuff?
99. Are you genderfluid or have another sexual orientation than straight?

Social interaction

Differences between autistic and neurotypical communication styles

Issues with social interaction are at the core of autism because we struggle to understand cues, body language, tone of voice and other things that neurotypical people seem to get intuitively when talking to each other. It can feel like someone wrote a detailed guide on social interaction but forgot to share it with us.

Trouble with connecting socially is often the reason we think we're different from others. It can be a lonely, nagging feeling deep inside because we feel unable to connect with anyone. Or we can experience shameful and difficult scenes where others yell at us for making grave social mistakes. When we or our parents talk to a therapist or doctor for the first time, these are the incidents we'll highlight, and it's a big part of finding our diagnosis.

But have you considered that there might be nothing wrong with us socially? I'm not claiming that we're all the same as neurotypicals, because we're clearly not. But it doesn't mean there's something fundamentally wrong with the way we communicate. It's just different, and that creates trouble when neurotypicals try to understand us and we them.

When you read articles about the symptoms of autism, it seems like our ability to communicate properly is broken. But it's not, and it doesn't necessarily need to be fixed. As autistic people have been trying to tell the research and medical community for a long time, we communicate just fine with each other. The communication doesn't break down until you throw a neurotypical person into the mix.

But how can we test that? Dr Catherine Crompton, who is a research neuropsychologist in Scotland, has started to share some details from an ongoing and yet unpublished study she has been doing on the efficiency of autistic people's communication skills.

She has recruited groups of neurotypicals and autistic people to participate in different communication tasks. One of the things she has done is asking a group of people to get a message from one person to another. The message has to go through everyone before it reaches the last person, and how much of the original message is conveyed to the last person is then analysed.

Not surprisingly, the groups of neurotypicals did this just fine, and the mixed groups of neurotypicals and autistic people performed poorly. However, the groups consisting only of people on the spectrum did just as well as the group consisting of neurotypicals. So the communication lines don't break down because autistic people are inefficient or do anything wrong. They break down because autistic people and neurotypicals don't communicate in the same way (Crompton, 2019).

Dr Crompton and her fellow researchers also interviewed people participating about how they felt during the experiment. And when asked about their experience, autistic people and neurotypicals were equally frustrated when they had been told to communicate with each other.

Some conversations between participants were also videotaped and then analysed for social cues and rapport. From those videos, it seems like other people observing the conversations think people on the spectrum actually have greater rapport amongst themselves than the neurotypicals do (Crompton, 2019).

This doesn't come as a great surprise to me. To be honest, my impression from speaking with other autistic people is that we're in general better at giving a direct message. We have such a great ability to be honest and to consider the words that are being said without thinking that there's a hidden message somewhere, or that the other person has ulterior motives. All that trouble usually starts when a neurotypical person tries to read things into what we're saying. But since there are more neurotypicals than autistic people, no one questions their ability to communicate properly.

We say what we mean, and we mean what we say. If we wanted to tell you something else, we would have done that. If we all base more of our communication on facts and skip the small talk, we would probably be a happier and more efficient society.

Still, I think it's very helpful to go through the differences in communication style and discuss both the issues and advantages we can have when communicating with others. And of course I welcome all further research on the topic to explore this further, since one small study isn't by far enough to prove anything.

Being non-verbal

One of the first things you'll find when reading about someone on the spectrum is that some of us don't speak with others at all. This is usually said in an effort to explain that someone with autism can be non-verbal.

It doesn't mean that they don't communicate though. And there are many other ways of communicating than just talking. Many can use body language, sign language, pictures, and some can write or even sing.

People who are non-verbal are often also rated as "more autistic" which doesn't have to be the case, as autism is a spectrum and not a line from best to worst. But I understand how it can be very difficult for someone to live in a world where they have trouble participating in spoken conversations.

Some autistic people will also speak, but not construct sentences on their own. Perhaps they will only repeat words or phrases spoken by others, something that's called echolalia. Some again will have selective mutism where they talk in some situations and not in others. Often can a meltdown trigger someone to stop talking for a while.

No one has yet to find an explanation to why some people on the spectrum are non-verbal, but there are several suggested theories ranging from too many sensory inputs to co-occurring learning disorders.

Body language

We also tend to have difficulties reading other people's body language. This can cause trouble when we try to interpret what other people mean or feel, as a lot of information is conveyed through how they hold their body. For example will most neurotypicals who are annoyed or bored not tell you directly, but they will show it with their body language.

I find that I often struggle with placing orders or talking to someone to get a short task done if they don't stick to the script I expect. And if they don't spell out what they want, we end up in a stance where they think they're waiting for me to say something, while I'm waiting for them to tell me what they need. They're using their body language to signal that's it my turn to talk or that they need more information from me, but unless they say it, I won't pick up on it.

Another type of body language autistic people often will have trouble with is direct eye contact. There are two sets of theories explaining why we don't seek out other people's eyes as frequently as neurotypicals do. One is that we're not particularly interested in other people and don't care that much about the information we can get from looking into someone's eyes. The other is that it's too intense for us to look directly at someone, so it takes away our ability to focus on other things.

It could also be a combination of both. I remember being 16 and explaining to a boy I was seeing that I had just learnt that you could flirt with someone just by looking at them. It was the very first time I had really thought about eye contact.

In general, I'll always avoid eye contact in emotional settings, which has bothered several boyfriends. But I have become pretty good at looking people in the eyes regularly, although it still feels very intense.

If it feels overwhelming to you, there is no need to force yourself to look someone in the eyes. You can either explain that you're not comfortable with eye contact, or you can look somewhere close to their eyes so they think they're looking at them. But the latter is a form of masking, so only do that if you really want to.

Rigid thinking

People on the spectrum often tend to think that there's only one solution to a problem, and if they have one interpretation of something, there can't be another. This can lead to conflicts with others because they feel we refuse to see something from their point of view.

It can also be difficult for us to do simple things like filling out forms or answer someone's questions because we think that the premises are inaccurate. Most people I know will just answer whatever is easiest for them. But if something isn't 100% correct, I'm not comfortable writing it, and I think many autistic people struggle with the same thing.

I'm the only one in my office who struggle with additional paperwork with my bank because I'm a tax resident in more than one country, even though most of my colleagues are as well. The questionnaire wasn't clear, so instead of just filling out the same that everyone else did, I had a tax lawyer draft a lengthy letter explaining the differences to the bank. This led to more problems, more paperwork, and it didn't solve anything. None of my colleagues ever did any of these things. But I couldn't simplify my answers on one single form, and I ended up with months of extra work and legal costs to get it right.

When it comes to rigid thinking, there are several exercises that are suggested to use with autistic children so they can learn from early on that there can be more than one way to find a solution. After you think of one way to solve a problem, you can think about how it could have been solved differently, or how other alternatives would have also been acceptable. That way, we can train ourselves to accept that other people have different views from our own.

Black and white thinking

I think black and white thinking can be seen together with rigid thinking and our need to seek the truth and nothing else. We think that something is either right or wrong. This is often viewed as a weakness, but I don't fully agree with that.

Some things might have grey areas, but others don't. And too many people can't be bothered to find out if something is correct or not. They think that the answer will always lie somewhere in the middle of two people's point of view, even when that isn't the case. I hate it when someone says that we should "agree to disagree," because I would never agree to say that something is just a difference of opinion when it's actually a fact – and it's wrong.

I think the strong conviction we have about how to do something can lead us to find solutions where other people give up or take shortcuts. We should stay true to our abilities to seek clear answers and to our strong sense of right and wrong.

Telling the truth

Another issue that makes autistic women unpopular in some settings is our honesty. We tend to hate to lie, even if it's a white lie. I think that learning to exchange niceties about someone's hair or clothes can be good. But otherwise, being able to see the truth is a strength.

It has been said that we feel more connected to facts and truth than to other people. We're logical beings, and we should use that for all it's worth. Too many people are caught up in lies and pretending just for pretending's sake, but we don't have to be a part of it.

One of the things my husband loves about me is that I always tell the truth. It doesn't mean I actively seek out people to tell them negative things about them, but if we're having a discussion, I'll give my honest opinion.

It also gives us a great strength when it comes to changing our opinions, which many people refuse to do. If we're trying to find the truth, and it turns out something we used to believe is wrong, we can change. Ask my husband. I used to refuse to wash vegetables and fruit when I moved to London because I thought the water in the sink was dangerous since it tasted so awful. He kept telling me that the risk of getting sick from eating unwashed fruit was a lot higher than the risk of ever getting sick from the tap water. I thought he was wrong, but when I fact-checked it, it turned out he was right. And I now clean all my vegetables with distasteful London water before eating them.

Since we don't tend to lie, we can also struggle to understand both when and why other people lie. It can be frustrating not to see how people change their body language when they tell us something that's untrue. And since we tell the truth, we don't necessarily look for other people to lie either.

I wish I would have been better at recognising other people's false claims and stories, but unfortunately, I'm not. However, I wouldn't have wanted to become someone who lies just to get access to that neurotypical ability.

Small talk never happens

Small talk must be one of the things that's universally disliked by everyone on the spectrum. Not only do we have to read the body language of people we don't know and make conscious decisions about what to say, but we have little control over the topic of the conversation and can end up boring ourselves to death.

I've learnt a few standard questions that are suitable for small talk, but whenever the conversation continues down the same track, I get so bored I fall off. It's easy to start talking about the weather, social events or non-invasive topics. But it's so dull. And since I'm autistic, I tend to have very strong opinions, and I can end up offending people over the most benign things.

There are some instances at work when I have to endure small amounts of small talk, but in my personal life, I do anything to avoid it. I want to remove myself from any situations where people enjoy discussing real estate prices, Brexit, or the social agenda of the season. I also tend to doze off if people start name-dropping or talk about self-care as if it's a new religion.

On the positive side, we often have a lot of knowledge in areas of interest to us, and we can give completely new perspectives on topics that people often find difficult to talk about.

I want to discuss matters of deep love, fear of death, nuances in 2008 Champagne, women's rights, or the meaninglessness in Albert Camus' books. I try to use this as motivation to go to events where I know small talk will be required. Because if you start talking to someone and dare to take chances, you can find a person who has the same weird interests as you. I've been lucky enough to do that more than once.

At a party, you can end up with that one other person who feels the same way and who loves the way you think. Deep friendships and meaningful conversations even with strangers are some of the things I enjoy that I don't think I would have had the opportunity to experience if I didn't think a bit differently from most people and chose to step outside the boundaries of normal small talk from time to time. Dare to have interesting conversations and run away from the people who only want to talk about the news.

__Oversharing__

Even though we're often shy and introverted, we can have a tendency to overshare or become too personal too quickly. There are several ways this can happen.

One is the classical "info-dumping" where we won't stop talking about our special interests. If I'm having dinner with someone, I tend to dominate the conversation whenever there's wine on the table, and if other people let me, I'll discuss grape varieties all night long.

But although this makes me slightly boring in other people's eyes, it doesn't necessarily mean they think I'm awkward. But I also tend to share too many personal details with people I don't know well enough. Sometimes to the extent that the people listening get embarrassed.

I went out for drinks with a woman that was new at my firm. She was extremely cool and came from an interesting business background. Since I had very few female colleagues at the time, I was super excited to have someone to bond with.

Over a few glasses of wine, I ended up sharing details of getting divorced, and I told her about all my dating failures in London. I didn't realise that she hadn't shared the same amount with me until she joked about it next week in the office. Luckily, it wasn't ill-spirited on her end, but I still felt a wave of shame running over my entire body. At that moment, I understood that I had shared too much because I so desperately wanted her to like me and be my friend.

After that incident, we didn't end up becoming close, and I still believe she thinks I'm weird because of what I told her that evening. But it doesn't always end up like that. The closest friends I have are also people I overshared with the first few times I met them, and it brought us together.

Sharing intimate details and being passionate quickly is something I see as a strength for someone with autism, but in matters of work, it might be taken the wrong way.

I have made it a rule for myself that I try to not have personal relationships at work, and I limit alcohol at work dinners. I don't say that everyone should do that, but it's what I've found helpful since I work in a very conservative industry.

Tone and nuances

Nuances coming from tone of voice are often lost on people on the spectrum, and some of us struggle understanding jokes and sarcasm. I think several of these misunderstandings are also caused by the fact that we tend to take things more literally than they're meant.

I'm pretty bad at sarcasm according to neurotypical people in my life. I can make sarcastic jokes, and while I understand some of my really close friends' humour, it's completely lost on me if my husband makes a joke. Many of the people I've dated over the years have complained that I don't understand their jokes or sarcasm at all. Personally, I believe this has more to do with me not thinking what they say is funny, so I don't understand why someone would make a joke about it.

I think we also tend to say exactly what we mean without hiding anything else in our tone of voice. Therefore, *we* get confused when other people expect us to find nuances in what they say. And *they* get confused when they try to look for hidden meanings in what we say or do.

Taking things literally

Since we don't catch all the little nuances from a change in tone or body language, it's only natural that we pay more attention to the words people say. But when we do, we assume that all the information someone wants to give us is in the words of the sentences. If they say something, we take it for what it is. We take things literally.

This can lead to a few misunderstandings when neurotypicals think we understand what they mean, but they're really saying something completely different. Most of these situations are quite funny in retrospect. One friend of mine in college used to joke that if someone would claim that "love was in the air," I would interrupt saying "No, the air consists of Nitrogen, Oxygen and Carbon Dioxide."

When my husband and I was having some nice turbot at an Icelandic fish restaurant, I kept talking about how good it was. He looked at me and said: "You should add turbot your list of fish." I replied confused: "My list of fish? But I can't remember any lists I have that go particularly into fish."

Since I write lists for everything, I kept scanning my memory to try to find a fish list. But it turned out he meant a figurative list, and that adding it to my list meant that it was a type of fish I enjoyed eating. We both laughed when we realised what had happened, but that isn't always the case.

Although it's sometimes funny, many people can be extremely offended by corrections or by someone taking something literally. There's one experience that I've told almost no one about because it makes me feel sick to my stomach every time I think about it. I was in my mid-20s, and I had just gotten married to my first husband and moved to a new city with him where I knew very few people. This meant I came with him to parties and social gatherings so I could meet new friends.

One evening, we were together at a house party with some of his friends, and I knew no one there. I was drinking, which often makes me feel at ease in social situations. It can make me participate more in conversations, and at the time, I felt I really needed that.

I was sitting at a table having a conversation with a woman

and a man. The guy worked in sales for an electronics company and was talking about cellphone attributes. He was trying to make a point saying that people only consider the positive aspects of a phone when buying a new one, and not the negative parts. I thought that sounded like a really odd thing to claim, so I asked him to support this. He then proceeded to make a really off point where he thought that the word attribute meant that something could only be positive. I saw where his argument was headed and said he didn't need to go there because it still wouldn't prove his point, so he should try to make another one.

This made the guy explode. He yelled at me that I was a stupid Aspergers' whore that should keep to myself. I was really surprised and stuttered that I thought we had been having a nice discussion for the past hour. The woman who had been sitting quietly at the other side of the table then decided that her first contribution to the conversation would be to say that I was a horrible person who had only been saying mean and argumentative things all night. I took it really personally, went up to my husband and tried to say that I wanted to leave, but I wasn't able to say anything. I started crying and ran out in the hallway.

I left the party alone and wandered around alone in the city for quite some time before I went home. It was humiliating, and I felt like a social failure that would never be able to make new friends. I had only tried to tell him what he said really meant, and apparently, he wasn't ok with that.

Correcting mistakes

My previous story also goes into the next topic, which is correcting other people's mistakes. For some reason, when neurotypicals say something, they don't like to be corrected. I find that weird, as I would like to find out if I had any misconceptions, especially about something I'm interested in. But for neurotypicals, this breaks their social code, and they think it's a personal attack.

If you don't have any issues understanding this concept, it might sound funny to you, but I didn't realise it until quite recently. And most of the social mistakes I've made by correcting people have ended pretty badly.

I'm quite good at remembering things, and I read up on new subjects with passion and excitement. This means that if I talk about something, I usually know that what I'm saying is right.

When I correct someone, I don't mean it in a bad way, I just want the other person to have the right information. Holding it back is actually physically painful. My only solution if I'm not saying something, is to completely disengage from the conversation, and maybe plaster on a fake smile that looks pretty horrible.

At my first job, a woman working at HR wanted to have a conversation with me because she was worried I didn't get along with some of the women in the other departments. She was referring to a dinner we went to where we were ordering a few bottles of wine for the table. One of the women there made some casual remarks about Cava and Prosecco. I corrected her, trying to explain the difference in production methods, and apparently, she was really offended by it.

Perhaps I shouldn't have said anything, but I didn't understand that, because I was so focused on getting everyone the right information. I would have been perfectly fine drinking the Prosecco, just as long as everyone was aware of what the differences between the two bottles were.

I've had similar experiences where people have gotten really mad at me. When I was around 13, an older girl on my swim team complained about a trigonometry problem she faced in school. I thought I would help her, and said that the problem she was talking about wasn't very hard. I then told her to solve it by measuring one of the angles, calculate the missing side in the triangle and solve for the rest.

She got furious, and one of the other girls had to tell her to calm down because it looked like she was going to physically attack me. She said that I didn't know any better than to make stupid comments like that. I felt hurt by both. I didn't feel like my comment was stupid. In fact, I just helped her solve a problem she was struggling with at school.

That's one of the many times I've learnt that if it's one thing neurotypical people hate even more than being corrected by someone much younger than themselves, it's being told that something they think is difficult is easy for others.

I've tried to understand why neurotypicals and autistic people are so different in this area. I think it might be because some neurotypicals use corrections as a way to show off their power over someone or to humiliate them. While most autistic people are just very eager to find out what's right, and we want to share that with everyone else.

<u>Timing</u>

Something that made my doctor laugh when I first mentioned that I thought I was autistic, was that I interrupted him in the middle of a sentence to list all my symptoms. We were talking on the phone, and I quickly added: "yes, I also interrupt people." Since autistic people have trouble catching the dynamics neurotypical people have in their conversations, it can be hard for us to understand when it's our turn to speak.

In meetings, I often find that I either never get a word in because someone else starts talking, or I end up interrupting. Sometimes, I also think that people are about to stop, or that because they said something that needs clarification from me, they want me to step in and comment on that immediately. Often they don't.

I hate being interrupted myself, so I should have sympathy for others when I'm the one talking over them. And I've learned to apologise for interrupting, either before I start talking or afterwards. It's also polite to ask the person who was speaking before you to please go on with what they were saying, and it helps to be able to laugh at yourself when you're interrupting.

I think it's a strength that we have strong opinions that we want to convey right away, but we should understand that it annoys other people. If we're uncomfortable interrupting, we can also try to wait for silence and then add our opinions when everyone else is done.

Being overwhelmed in groups

If you're like me, you're able to hold a pretty decent conversation if you're talking to one person alone. Especially if you're discussing something that's of relative interest to both of you.

I'm also able to give a good first impression in a job interview or a meeting. The setting is familiar, and we have a fixed set of things to discuss during the time we're together. Body language can be learnt, and I try to add nods, eye contact and mimicking the other person's posture.

The trouble starts when you introduce other things into the mix. If you're trying to be social within a larger group, it gets very hard to keep track of what people are saying and how they're acting. The easy thing is to drop out of the conversation because all your energy goes to interpreting what's happening around you.

I find that I shut off if I'm in a big group, even if I compensate with alcohol. The easiest thing for me to do is to try to create a more private setting with only one of the other participants. If you're at a party where people can move around freely, this is often easy. If you're in a classical networking situation where people talk in groups, or at a big dinner where everyone is expected to participate in the same conversation, it gets harder.

If I put all my energy to it, I can mask for a while in a group, but it can exhaust me for days afterwards. Working so hard to be something I'm not, isn't worth it to me. I find that it's better to either find a group of people who understand your autistic quirks or to not attend those types of group functions. We shouldn't have to risk our health just to please a lot of people in a room.

Masking

If you've never heard of masking in the context of autistic women before, the title of this sub-chapter probably confused you. Masking is the act of changing your natural behaviour to cover up your autistic traits. It's referred to as "masking" because we're putting on a mask to do something that doesn't come naturally to us.

This can be anything from stopping yourself from stimming, talking about things you don't care about, mimicking body language and speech, forcing eye contact, faking emotions and facial expressions, or taking on a completely different personality. Making up rules and practising lines ahead of a conversation are also common techniques to survive socialising in the neurotypical world.

According to Tony Attwood, who is a world-renowned autism expert, autistic women often try to fit in with the neurotypical world by running pre-made scripts in conversations and by mimicking other people. They also use raw intelligence to decipher social rules and situations (Attwood, 2006).

We rehearse conversations in our heads. We repeat those we've already had to trace our mistakes and think about other ways of saying it, and we think about the ones we're going to have so we can plan what to say. When we do or say something wrong, we think about it for days or weeks, and we're not able to let anything go. We try so hard to fit into society's expectations of women as social butterflies, that we cover up our real selves until there's nothing left.

Both men and women use techniques to mask, but women do it more than men (Lai et al., 2016). Reasons for masking are many. Wanting to fit in, getting a job, and making friends are all mentioned as motivation for actively wanting to camouflage symptoms of autism (Hull et al., 2017).

Several of the women in the UK qualitative study I mentioned in the second chapter reported that they felt like they were wearing a mask or took on a different persona to fit in. This was especially the case when they were younger. Some even reported actively using books, magazines or movies to learn how to act like someone else in certain situations. Alcohol was also reported as something used to be able to come across as a "normal" person (Bargiela et al., 2016).

I spent a lot of time reading women's magazines and watching stupid American comedies when I was younger because I thought it would teach me how to act around others. And if I saw a woman that was well-liked, beautiful and confident, I would try to understand what made her that way. One time, I even thought that if I learnt how to whistle through my fingers, I would be as cool as the girl who was dating the boy I secretly liked.

Because of all this active training, I was able to pass as a neurotypical quite often. But that didn't do me any favours. My confidence was at its lowest, as I thought if people found out who I really was, they would hate me. If I ever let my mask slip, they would never speak to me again because they would realise what a social weirdo I was. It wasn't until I was in my mid-twenties that I started exploring who I was behind all of this, and tried to see if that person might be likeable as well.

But masking and following social rules have given me some good things in life. I have a very good job, and at the moment, very few of the people I work with know that I have an official autism diagnosis, although everyone knows I'm a bit different.

For some autistic people, their ability to mask can be seen as a huge success. Proud parents, teachers or therapist say they have "conquered autism" and can go on to live a happy, neurotypical life with their peers. But masking comes at a very steep price. It takes a lot of energy to actively analyse all social situations to find out what to do. Exhaustion is one of the most frequent results from masking (Hull et al., 2017). Just think about the amount of rest you need after pulling through an entire evening of small talk over dinner. Doing this every day will eventually make you hit the wall and collapse. This is what we call autistic burnout, and it's no joke.

If you're good at masking, you also risk not getting a proper diagnosis until you're well into adulthood. You might struggle to be believed or taken seriously if you try to discuss issues you have in your social life because to the outside world, you seem to do it all naturally.

And this behaviour starts early. Even in childhood, masking can be noticed in schoolyards when autistic girls try to follow or mimic the neurotypical children. Girls on the spectrum will for example go in and out of activities with other children to avoid making obvious social mistakes. First, they will watch until they think they understand how to act, but when they feel uncertain again, they will leave so no one discovers that they don't know the rules. While boys on the spectrum are more likely to play alone (Dean et al., 2017).

Because it seems like they're getting along with other kids just fine, it makes it less likely that teachers or parents pick up on girls' behaviour early.

In many instances, people think that smart and autistic women have an easier life because they're able to mask their symptoms, or they're able to learn rules that stop them from making mistakes. In some cases, that can be true. But in many ways, I think it's just another layer of something that makes us feel different from everyone else.

This is why I so desperately need to explain to you as a reader, that when I make suggestions about what you can do in social situations, or point out differences between us and neurotypicals, I don't mean that you should stop being you and become a different person who can master all these rules. I simply think it's better for us if we're aware of when we can get misunderstood and then make our choices accordingly. So please don't take this as a guide on how to mask your autistic traits to become someone you're not.

When you mask by putting on someone else's personality, you risk losing yourself. Meaning you don't really know what your preferences are if someone asks you, because you're so used to trying to figure out what's expected of you socially instead of trusting your own opinion. It can go so far that you have multiple personalities, but you have no sense of self.

In my early twenties, I remember being frustrated whenever people made comments like "I'm so spontaneous" or "I love going out." How could they just know all of these things about themselves?

I felt like a new boyfriend or a new school meant a new set of interests or a new personality for me. Did my boyfriend love hunting? Sure, I'll learn how to use a shotgun. Was he an avid traveller? I would love to go on any trips he suggested. And the things I liked to do, like writing, drinking nice wine or playing tennis were almost completely abandoned during my search for something that would get me to fit into someone else's life.

This continued even to the point of speaking differently or using other mannerisms. I've never lived in the US, but I have an American accent after an American boyfriend, and at some point, I also had an accent from the other side of Norway because I was with a man who spoke like that. It didn't end until we broke up and one of my friends asked me to please start speaking normally again.

In the end, you can feel like all your relationships are built on a lie. If you believe that your true personality is too horrible to show others, you'll constantly live in fear of being found out. It's extremely stressful, and it tears your self-esteem to pieces.

It's an empty feeling. And it's lonely. The only way back is to start the process of figuring out who you are and accept what you find. If some people won't be a part of your life anymore because of that, it's probably worth leaving them behind if it means you can become more comfortable with yourself.

When I started the process of figuring out who I was, it took me a long time to realise which interests and opinions were actually mine to begin with. But it was all worth it, and I don't think I would have been able to be in a healthy relationship today had I not taken that time for self-discovery.

Friendships

I never feel as alone as when I'm surrounded by people chatting and smiling. They see each other, but they don't see me. And when I do my best to take on a visible form, they quickly realise I'm not one of them. When I start talking to someone, I'm just waiting for them to realise that I'm not like them. Not likeable or mouldable. I'm rigid and mean. I can't hide my feelings, although it feels like I've spent my entire life hiding.

It's not that I don't want friendships. But they're difficult to get and take too much energy to keep. Friendships can be the ultimate test for your social skills. They can be beautiful and trusting, and they can also develop from uncomplicated childhood games to drama and hurt feelings.

Friendships change as we grow older, and the rules tend to get more and more complex. At some point, women on the spectrum can fall off. This often happens at the point in time during childhood when easily structured playfulness turns into social games with a new set of rules that no one explains to us.

In general, I have the impression that women on the spectrum are less eager to play social games and chitchat, which can make it difficult for us to make friends as adults. We're avoiding some of the things people do to meet others, and we can be seen as rude or mean because we don't follow social norms and expectations.

That doesn't mean our relationships are any less important, but we make connections differently than neurotypicals. We build lasting friendships based on common interests. And when we find people we can be ourselves around, we take our masks off and make friends for life.

A small study done in a US high school with an autism program showed that autistic people were much more likely to have a best friend who was also on the spectrum. When asked about what was important for them in a friendship, they listed trustworthiness, someone they could talk to, patience and someone they could relate to (Locke et al., 2010).

These are things we could expect to find in other autistic people, and things we recognise in ourselves. So we have a tendency to find each other and make friends. We stand out in a group, and we don't always fit in with neurotypicals. But we can still build strong and meaningful relationships with each other.

I don't have a huge network of friends that I go out for drinks with every day after work, but I have some extremely good friends that I've met in different phases of my life. They consist of both men and women, and although they're all different as individuals, they have a few things in common.

They're sensitive and thoughtful people who appreciate complete honesty, and we can fall out of touch for months at a time without losing any intimacy when we talk again. When we speak or see each other, we go straight to the core of the most important things. I know I can reach out to them if I need someone to listen to me or to set me straight, but we don't necessarily need all the social contact that many people think are mandatory to uphold a friendship.

Some of these people are on the spectrum. Some are just not neurotypical. They're all extremely smart, and some of them are also at times vulnerable. Like me. And the hard things I've been through in my life make me equipped to be there for them during difficult times. When they see the world differently; I do too.

Friendships are invaluable for women on the spectrum. That they don't always look like what you thought they would, shouldn't get you down. Less social contact doesn't mean less quality for the contact you have.

Women on the spectrum are loyal and forceful, and anyone should be happy to have them on their team. We might need to realise we're never going to be the most popular people in school or at work, but we're perfectly capable of having long-term friendships in our lives.

Online friendships and social media apps have also made it easier for us to stay in touch with friends without being subject to pressure or needing to spend time with someone for three hours at a time to make it count.

Some women on the spectrum have reported that they have an easier time being friends with men because society lets them act more freely and straight-forward. But I think there's something special about becoming friends with other women who are like you.

And if you think that you don't have anyone in your community to befriend, there are other ways to meet similar people. Many women find friendships with other women on the spectrum through online groups, for example on Facebook (Bargiela et al., 2016).

If you haven't already, I suggest you reach out to a few groups on Facebook. You can search for autism or Asperger's, and you can find groups for women only if that makes you feel safer. Most groups are closed, but it's easy to be added. You can find people to meet up with in your area, or you can share your interests or get support from others online.

Self-work

These exercises are divided into two parts. First, I want you to spend some time analysing your current behaviour to find out if you're masking. Then, I want you to make conscious decisions about which social behaviours you're happy with, and what you want to change. That part you have to do yourself, but I'm providing some examples of the rules I have built for myself.

Are you masking:
1. Do you rehearse conversations that aren't hugely important?
2. Do you get angry with yourself for several days if you

make one social mistake?
3. Do you act very differently when you're with separate groups of people?
4. Do you tend to mimic social cues or even the dialect of the person you're talking to?
5. Are you dependent on wearing a certain type of clothes or makeup before you're comfortable in public?
6. Do you always say yes to what other people suggest?
7. Do you read magazines or books to try to learn how to act and use body language?
8. Do you feel that you're hiding something when you talk to friends?
9. Are you exhausted after short amounts of socialising?
10. Are you relieved when social events are cancelled?
11. Do you apologise for things you say all the time?
12. Do you smile when you're not genuinely happy?
13. Do you have pre-made sentences you run through for different situations?
14. Do you mimic characters you see in movies?
15. Does your dialect ever change?
16. Do you avoid saying things you find funny out loud?
17. Is it difficult for you to describe yourself with five words?
18. If someone asks a question in a group, do you wait to answer until you can hear what the other people say?
19. Do you wait long to say something because you need to think through different ways of saying it first?
20. Are you constantly afraid that people will find out who you really are?

The more you feel like these things describe you, the more likely it is that you're using some form of masking to get through life. Consider if you're comfortable doing that or if you want to get to know yourself better and show more of who you are to friends.

Then continue to find out which social rules you want to follow. You can use my examples, or you can write down rules you've found to be helpful in your own life already.

Rules for socialising:

1. Always use please and thank you generously. Use it whenever you ask for something or when you're given something. I struggled with these as a teenager, as the expressions are less common in Scandinavian culture, but I find they give a nice structure to any conversation.
2. If you want to be in rapport with someone, you can look at how they hold their body. If they get closer, you can get closer, and if they pull away you can do the same. If you want someone to understand that you don't like them, you can do the opposite of what they do and pull away. No matter what, always stay with what's comfortable for you.
3. You don't need to give someone unsolicited advice like asking them to shower more often unless this is someone you're very close with and it bothers you.
4. If someone says something wrong, you don't have to correct them unless it's detrimental to the conversation. You can decide that you want to move on and talk to someone else or about something else instead.
5. If you feel like it drains your energy to argue with someone who is wrong, you can try to have an inner dialogue with yourself about how important it is for you to pursue the discussion. Maybe you're comfortable writing down what you think and not share it with him or her if you don't want to spend time and effort on an

argument.
6. An easy way of surviving small talk is to ask people questions about themselves. Most people love talking about their interests, and you might get to dig deeper into an interesting topic they mention.
7. Remember what people have told you about their weekend plans and holidays, and ask them how it was when they come back from it so they know that you pay attention to what they tell you. It might not be important or interesting to you, but it can be important to them.
8. Give compliments freely.
9. If you're much more comfortable in individual conversations than groups, try to structure events so you get to talk to only one person at a time. Maybe you attend a more unstructured dinner party where people sit at small tables and are free to move around, or maybe you socialise with your colleagues by going out for lunch with only one person.
10. Don't ever feel pressured to extend socialising longer than you're comfortable with. You don't have to give people excuses if you're not up for anything. You can let them know that it's not a good time, or that you want time for yourself. You don't owe anyone an explanation, and it's fine to say you have to leave after two hours and stick to it.

Changes and details

Attention to detail

Temple Grandin, who is a famous autistic author and professor of animal science, writes in her book "Thinking in pictures" that she has a different way of processing thoughts than most people. Instead of thinking in words, she sees pictures or entire movies playing in her head.

Grandin also believes she has identified three distinct ways the autistic brain works. We either process information through pictures, words or patterns (Grandin, 2006). Each of the three profiles has their own distinct set of abilities, but the thing they all have in common is that they're very detail-oriented.

I couldn't pick one of these profiles if anyone asked me, and I believe we're more complex than using only one way of thinking. But I can see myself using both patterns, words, numbers and pictures. Sometimes alternating, sometimes together. However, the main way it feels like my mind works is by looking for a natural state of flow.

If I create or read a sentence that flows, I can feel it in my entire body like a deep intuition. If it doesn't flow, or something small is out of place, I can feel it everywhere as well, and it's physically unpleasant.

And no matter how I think, I always seem to have extremely good attention to detail. If something is out of place, if it doesn't follow an expected pattern, or if it doesn't work as it should, I notice, and I care.

Our superior attention to detail has been demonstrated in several studies. Autistic people are better at identifying hidden figures inside larger shapes (Jolliffe & Baron-Cohen, 1997), can identify continuity errors in films (Smith & Milne, 2009) and generally have superior auditory and visual perception (Mottron et al., 2006).

There's no single model that's able to explain why we're like that. Because here we are, the supposedly dysfunctional. The ones that think in an untraditional way, and in so many areas are considered to be less, not just different. Suddenly we're showing off ways in which our brains work more efficiently than neurotypical brains.

But some people think that we pay a steep price for our greater than average attention to detail. In the 80s and 90s, researchers tried explaining our outperformance on these tests by claiming we were unable to see the bigger picture and understand the full meaning of something. Because we were caught up in the small details, we were supposedly incapable of drawing conclusions from one situation to another if the two scenarios weren't identical, and we would miss out on everything else.

Our inability to see see the bigger picture and understand context has been named the "weak central coherence theory."

And according to researchers Francesca Happé and Uta Frith, this was long thought to be a driving force for several of the social difficulties people on the spectrum had.

The phenomenon was further explained by saying autistic people lacked "theory of mind," meaning we're unable to put ourselves in another person's position and understand how to see a situation from their point of view.

Not much later, however, people started realising that lack of central coherence wasn't necessarily correlated with weak theory of mind. After going through existing research on the subject, Happé and Frith suggested that even though there's strong evidence that autistic people have superior performance on tasks that require attention to detail, it doesn't necessarily mean they have a corresponding weaker understanding of the bigger picture (Happé and Frith, 2006).

From my personal experience, it's not that we're unable to understand how the small details tie into something bigger. It's that it's very difficult to move onto something else if we see a detail that doesn't make sense, and we want to make sure we fix that detail first.

When I was a child, I loved playing with lego. I would build beautiful houses by following the recipe that came with the box, step by step. Pretty much like an IKEA catalogue for kids. Sometimes, in the middle of building something, time would stand still for me. It was as if this sudden rage was flowing through my body. I would swear, scream, crush the houses I had built and then leave the lego for days. All of this was triggered if one small piece was missing. It didn't have to be something essential, the house could still have been built, but it would have a missing part.

To some extent, I still feel the same today. If one thing is out of place, everything else will be ruined. If I can't wear my planned outfit, a part of my jewellery is missing, or a gift I was supposed to give is gone, it feels like there's no point in doing what I had planned.

And I know that this is something that bothers both my neurotypical friends and my husband to no end. I sometimes can't think about the fact that I'm in a beautiful place and eating good food if the waiter gets my wine order wrong, or if someone misspells one of the main dishes on the menu. It's difficult to adjust, and I don't think I'll ever be able to let all smaller things go.

But I don't want to forget the beautiful aspects of it either. This example is more of a fun fact than anything else, but I would consider it a superpower because it's such an oddity. Whenever I go for a walk outside when I'm in the countryside, I find countless of four-leaf clovers. When I was a kid, I found hundreds of clovers with four, five, six or seven leaves. And so did my cousin, who was four years older than me and shared quite a lot of my other autistic traits.

As far as I know, no one has done any research on this topic in particular, and it probably isn't worth spending time on testing, but it seems as if this is an ability people on the spectrum share. I've seen this being discussed in several autism groups online as well, and I'm not the only one finding them or thinking there is a connection, although you might consider it wishful thinking.

For some reasons, our brains love to pick up on the change in patterns of the tiniest details in our surroundings. Since we also tend to focus more on objects than people, it's natural that we spend more time observing our environments.

If you search for videos of how to experience the world like an autistic person, you'll often find that they show us studying the sidewalk or something small and unimportant. It seems to take up a significant part of our attention. For me, that isn't a conscious process, but it's something my brain works out all on its own.

When I see a four-leaf clover, I don't always spot it right away. I feel like something with the pattern is different, and I sometimes turn and go back a few meters because it takes me some time to process it consciously.

I imagine that those abilities to pick up on patterns can be advantageous in jobs that have to do with design and finding aesthetically pleasing solutions. But I know it helps in my day-job as well, which mostly consists of building models, preparing powerpoint presentations and negotiating deals.

In so many jobs like law, finance, programming and design, attention to detail is the one thing you need to stand out from the crowd. That's also the case for painting, sewing, writing and drawing. You might be good, but to become extraordinary, you need an edge.

That edge can be your attention to smaller things that other people overlook. So although many people consider this to be a negative aspect of our personality, I would say it's one of our greatest strengths.

We might focus on one small detail and then forget the bigger picture for a while. And I can to some extent agree with the fact that this can make life harder for us in some instances where we put a lot more effort into something than we're supposed to. But when we're in charge of building something, and we can change that detail, we can create something unique and powerful.

Some researchers have already started to take this into account and have chosen to look for theories that are more about our strengths and differences than our weaknesses. For example does Simon Baron-Cohen think that our attention to detail comes from an ability to systemise. He sees that autistic people have a strong need and ability to both construct and analyse systems, and that this can be a great strength (Baron-Cohen,

2009).

What does that really mean? Well, there are several types of systems, but one thing they have in common is that they follow rules and they're predictable. We want to know everything there is about every detail. And while this means we sometimes miss the bigger picture because we're caught up in something, it also means that if we manage to control everything, we can understand it better than anyone.

So embrace this part of yourself instead of suppressing it. Nurture it if you need to, and don't be afraid of showing other people that this is who you are. They don't get to hold one of our biggest advantages against us.

Dependency on routines

The theory that autistic people are very strong at systemising might not explain every autistic trait, but it does say something about our need for routines, or what researchers also like to call "sameness." The routines can be to eat the same type of food, do things in a certain order, or simply do the same or see the same every day.

When something unexpected happens, even a small change, it can throw us completely off balance. This lies at the core of autism and is a part of the diagnostic criteria. But the routines or patterns are often described as being without any apparent meaning, and I think that part is wrong.

For us, there are many reasons why it makes sense to stick to a fixed routine. For example, if we don't like that something is wrong, or doesn't fit with the system, it's understandable that we don't like it when our routines are altered.

Other reasons why we prefer to stick to the same routine can be to reduce anxiety by having fewer inputs our brain needs to work with. Since we're already extremely sensitive to many sensory inputs, it's natural to believe that it can be difficult for us to deal with the added stress of routine changes.

But the fact is that we have yet to find a biological reason for why autistic people have such a strong need for routine in their lives. And neither researchers nor autistic people themselves seem to know exactly why we like to keep things a certain way. But most of us have entertaining examples of what happens when someone tries to change our environments against our will.

When I was a kid, I organised a demonstration against painting the kindergarten yellow. I even got one of the other girls to cry after berating her when she said she preferred the yellow colour.

The building had been white for the three years I had been there, and I saw no reason why that needed to change. I don't know why the change upset me so much. It wasn't the colour itself, and my bedroom at home was already yellow. But I was used to the building being white, and I had a strong need to keep it the way it was.

When I started school, I ate the same two pieces of bread for breakfast every day for years at a time. And I would have another two pieces for lunch. Not only did the bread stay the same, but I put the exact same things on it every day. In the morning it was my mother's jam without any lumps in it, and for lunch, I liked ham and paté. I would become extremely agitated if something changed, and a missing glass of milk could send me for a ride through rage.

I write as if this is all in the past, but it's still an issue, although somewhat smaller now that I'm aware of it. I eat the same for breakfast or lunch for a couple of months at a time. When I find something I enjoy, I prefer to stick with it for a while. Currently, I'm six-month into a love affair with microwaved porridge.

But I've learned that it's also ok to have days where I do something different. It either needs to be planned in advance, or I need to know that I can still opt out and follow my routine if I feel like it.

For example can this be to choose eating out with a colleague instead of having lunch at my desk. This could be perfectly fine for me, but if I planned to eat something and it's suddenly unavailable, I still get in trouble.

One recent example was when the cleaner threw out my pesto salad from the fridge because she thought the pesto was mouldy. I was suddenly out of food to eat, and even though I had plenty of places where I could go and pick up something, I wasn't in the mood. I had planned to eat that salad, and it took me a lot of willpower to not yell at people I worked with. Not until hours later when I suddenly caved and was hungry did I order something on Deliveroo.

For me, a routine change feels worse if there's no logical reason driving it. If I can see why we need to do it a different way today, then I can usually get by. If it's not, I get difficult.

Sometimes it doesn't even have to be a routine that I've had for a long time. If I'm handed a menu at a restaurant, make up my mind and then get told that the dish I wanted isn't on the menu anymore, I get annoyed. If they had told me when they handed me the menu, it would have been fine, but not when they offered it to me and then take it away. It also doesn't make sense if they say they can't make something because they're out of one key ingredient really early in the day, and this ingredient is readily available at a supermarket less than two minutes away. I need a reason, and I need logic. Without it, I can't be at ease.

Another big trigger is when my cleaner or my husband move any of my things. To be able to find things when I need them, they can't be moved by anyone else. It also interrupts my sense of logic, since there's usually a reason why I put something a specific place. If the other person had no logical reason for putting it somewhere else, it makes it even harder not to get triggered by it.

The combination of overwhelming sensory inputs and a change of routines can make my reaction even worse. One place where this often happens is when I travel.

Delays and changes can often happen unexpectedly and with little explanation. This causes a disruption in my plans, but it also forces me to stay even longer in an uncomfortable situation where people are noisy, smell weird and the environment is overstimulating.

The meltdowns I have when I travel are therefore stronger than usual. In addition, they can be very embarrassing because I'm having them in front of other people.

Whenever I fly, I like to have plenty of time to get to the airport, and I usually go in a car so I can be alone in a quiet space as long as possible. My husband on one occasion talked me into taking the train because he said it would be faster. But when we got to the train station, there was no train going at that time, and my husband hadn't checked the schedule.

We had to wait quite long for the next train, and we weren't sure we were going to make it to the airport on time. This made me extremely stressed, and I got so angry with him because he had managed to get me to break my routine without having checked that his option would work.

When the train arrived, it was full and noisy, and it finally made me crack. I yelled at my husband in front of an entire wagon of passengers. I could see his eyes get watery as people were staring at us, and I felt so warm, overwhelmed and horrible.

It made me so sad to see how he reacted, and I felt awful for doing it to him. We sat the entire train-ride in silence, but when we got off at the airport, I walked close to him, gave him a hug and whispered that I was sorry. He looked at me with loving and caring eyes and said he understood that I was upset and stressed, but that the way I reacted had made him extremely upset.

It still makes me depressed to think about it. This is, to me, one of the greatest downsides with being on the spectrum. We'll do things that hurt our friends and partners because we get overwhelmed and anxious, and we lash out in order to make it right. But instead of fixing it, we end up causing others pain.

With this in mind, I sound like both a bad wife, friend, and the most horrible train passenger in the world, but I'm not trying to be. And it's important to understand that routines and frameworks are something most people on the spectrum need, and not something we choose because we want to be difficult. It gives us peace and control in a world filled with so many things that bother us.

So what should we do when our need for routines is destroying good things in our lives? Most of the time, I try to change the world so that my routines won't get broken again, but I also understand the need to try to be more flexible. However, it's not always that easy to fix. It's a part of who we are, and if it was easy for us to change, we would probably not have been given the autism diagnosis in the first place.

I've found that having different routines for different situations is the best way for me to add flexibility. One routine for when I go out, another for when I'm home and in a hurry, and then another if I'm at home and have plenty of time. In the self-work section in this chapter, I've included some exercises for setting up alternative routines.

But we don't need to change a lot about ourselves, and I think the healthiest approach is to learn how to acknowledge our feelings of disappointment and loss of control when they occur.

Too often, autistic people are taught that their instincts are wrong and that they need to deal with the changes life throws at them and get over it. For example have most of us been trained to say that it doesn't matter when someone cancels on us.

But I don't think that saying this on autopilot is necessarily good for us. "It's all good, and we can reschedule," I've said too many times to dates or friends who have cancelled on me at the last minute.

We do this because we don't want to be seen as high maintenance, but inside we're hurting. Sometimes the anger and frustration we feel can be sensed by the other person, but we still hold it in to fulfil society's expectations.

One of the greatest things I've learnt is that it's ok to say that you're disappointed. You can do it without sounding angry, and you can say it's ok that you reschedule, but you're allowed to communicate that you're hurt. It makes it easier for us to process the disappointment, and we can share it with the other person in a better way than screaming at them.

It sounds very simple, but it was very powerful to me when I started using this technique. It lets me acknowledge my feelings towards the other person, and that made it easier for me to stay calm. When I try to hold it in, the resentment turns into anger and sometimes into a full-blown meltdown like with the train-ride to the airport.

When I've told the other person why I'm disappointed, I like to see if there are any positive things coming out of the change. Maybe I get extra time to spend at home because a friend cancels dinner plans at the last minute.

There's always something fun I could watch or read that I haven't had time for in a while, and it helps to do something I enjoy to get over the disappointment from the cancelled plans.

I also try to understand why the change needed to happen to see if there's any way I can prevent it in the future. If one friend is constantly unreliable, maybe I'll only make plans with that person if someone else comes along too. And if someone isn't good at making travel arrangements, I'll trust my own planning skills next time.

As with many of the issues for people on the spectrum, the need for routine isn't only negative. I try to spend time getting positive results from implementing good routines instead of getting stuck in patterns that aren't helpful long-term. When we know we have a strong need for keeping things the way they are, we might as well let our routines help us make healthy and logical choices each day.

Many of my routines are time and energy saving. If I know what to do in the morning every day, I don't need to ponder over what to have for breakfast or how I should plan my day. By building good core routines into your life, you can make it easy for yourself to accomplish big and long-term goals because your brain will make you do things automatically.

Eating the same type of meals are often used as examples of how you can lose weight with less effort. Tim Ferris (2011) even mentions it as one of the tools he uses in "The 4-Hour Body." He creates a few very good and nutritious meals, and then that's what he eats for long periods at a time. This is gold for someone on the spectrum who wants to have a healthy lifestyle. Just make sure that you build your routines consciously, so they end up taking you in the direction you want to go.

If you've ever read "The Power of Habit" (2012) by Charles Duhigg you'll understand how strong of a force habits are for almost all people. I suggest reading this book or something similar for you to truly acknowledge how strong the power of routines can be. They're hard to break, but if we're building up a habit to train, eat healthily or study a set amount of hours every day, this can get us through long-term challenges.

At the beginning of building a habit, you can see if there's a way to incorporate one of your hobbies or special interests (which I'll get back to in a separate chapter) into the new schedule you're building, or potentially use it as a carrot when you finish. When the habit is a part of your routine, you won't need that much effort to keep it up.

It can be helpful to try to identify the types of routines you rely on and what changes that annoy you. That way, you get to have a more conscious relationship with them, and you can work on including the habits you like and re-working those that make you struggle.

Self-work

The exercises in this chapter are centred around regulating your feelings when smaller details or routines are changed. And you should spend some time making conscious decisions about the routines you want to have in your life as well as figuring out what alternative strategies you can use when you're not able to follow them.

Identify your strengths and your triggers:
1. What small details do you notice that others don't?
2. How do you use logic to solve problems at work or in your personal life?
3. In what areas of your life does change make you uncomfortable?
4. What does it feel like when you see that something is out of place?
5. How do you communicate it to others if you notice that something is wrong?

6. What do you feel when plans are cancelled?
7. Are you good at recognising patterns in any area of life?

Build your own routines:

Describe your current routines for morning, afternoon and evening. What do you do and in what order? For each thing you do, ask yourself if it really belongs there and what it gives you as part of your routine. Then try to think of what you could have there instead, in case something stops you from doing that part of your routine one day.

1. Make a routine for everything you need to do between getting out of bed until you leave your house in the morning.
2. Make a routine for what you do between getting home, eating dinner and entertaining yourself or your family before bedtime.
3. Make a routine for everything you need to do to get ready for bed.

Make alternative routines ahead of time:

For each of the routines you've identified, try to figure out if you need several versions of it. If you do, you might want to make some alternatives ahead of time. For example, I like to have the following options for each of my most important routines:

1. How does your routine change when you have plenty of time?
2. How does your routine change if you don't have time to finish all of it?
3. How does your routine change if you're missing an ingredient or something else you need to complete it?
4. How does your routine change if you're doing it either alone or with someone else?

5. How does your routine change if you're travelling and have to do your routine in another city or country?

Sensory sensitivity

Hyper- or hyporeactivity to sensory input

Hyper- or hyporeactivity to sensory input is included in the DSM-5 as a part of autism spectrum disorder. When you are hyperreactive, you react too strongly to something, indicating that you are oversensitive. While if you are hyporeactive, you feel too little from sensory input.

For many women, myself included, the sensory difficulties that come along with autism are the things that bother us the most in daily life. That we react too strongly to something can also be what takes the longest to discover about ourselves.

By that, I don't mean that we won't know that harsh textures rubbing our skin feels horrible, or that a noisy day at work gives us crazy headaches. What we don't know is that other people don't feel the same way. Since we only have our own sensory inputs to rely on, we often don't notice that we feel things more or less intensely than others.

Like many before me, I assumed I was just not as good as friends, family or colleagues at tolerating noises, smells or touch. For a long time, I thought I needed to listen to some of my less sympathetic boyfriends and "toughen up." It never occurred to me that I was processing the world around me differently and that the challenges thrown at me therefore were harder.

The sensory sensitivity also made me doubt the possibility that I was autistic. I had the misconception that someone on the spectrum would automatically be less sensitive to everything around them. For a long time, I believed autism or Asperger's was about having fewer feelings and being less aware of the world. So when I started realising that my reactions to things around me were very strong, I never thought it could have anything to do with autism.

But the inverse is true. And although we don't know exactly what causes autistic people to react differently to sensory input, we know that it affects a great deal of both children and adults on the spectrum.

It could be that our senses experience the actual input as more or less intense, or that the sensory signals are interpreted differently by our brains. Another explanation is that we don't adapt our expectations about the world around us by using previous experiences.

The last theory I've found to be particularly interesting. But what does it actually mean? As you probably know, there are many examples of visual illusions where our brain tricks us into seeing something that isn't there. Some of these illusions will only affect us because our brain is applying all our prior knowledge about how the world works before it sends us an interpretation of what's in front of us.

Liz Pellicano and David Burr (2012), who are both cognitive scientists, suggest that autistic people don't apply the same amount of prior experience when interpreting sensory input. That we experience some things as if it was the very first time we interacted with them.

One could say that our experiences are more "pure" since we're not filtering out things based on our expectations. But it also means we spend more energy trying to understand and interpret what's happening without applying shortcuts. This could explain our need for trying to keep our surroundings constant and avoid disrupting our routines.

In her book, "Sensory Perceptional Issues in Autism and Asperger Syndrome," autism researcher Olga Bogdashina (2016) suggests that we should refer to different types of sensory experiences rather than characterise something as a sensory dysfunction. She even argues that several of the different sensory perceptions are more like super-abilities than dysfunctions.

Like Burr and Pelicano, she also points out that sensory overload can be the reason for several other problems people on the spectrum are facing. During an overload with too many sensory inputs, we shut down and retreat into our own worlds, or we try to stimulate our senses in a different way to make sense of it all.

I find this way of looking at sensory overload intriguing, and it's something I've thought myself as well. Some of my weirdest and most uncomfortable social experiences have happened while I've also been experiencing too intense sensory stimuli.

And isn't this the case for most of us when we're trying to be social? Social events are often held in places with a lot of noise. Not only from music or the surroundings, but from talking people. When we're trying to balance the noise, body odours and movements from people around us, there isn't much energy left to analyse the social situation itself.

I snap when there's too much going on around me at the

same time. And it feels more like a primal urge to protect myself than anything else. When others perceive me as crass, short or rude, I'm often just working hard to get my point across efficiently while at the same time battling the chaos around me. The impatience in my voice is the result of a wild chase where I have to keep running because there's no place to hide.

Unfortunately, the rest of the world lacks understanding of our sensory issues. And most people hesitate to offer us shelter because our desperate need for peace and quiet challenges their right to exist without compromise.

They misunderstand and think that we're weak, or that we're difficult primadonnas who ask too much of them. But we aren't weak. We're simply experiencing another reality than neurotypicals.

The world needs to be more accommodating to the needs of people on the spectrum. It's hard for us to navigate through all of this, and we can't protect ourselves from overstimulating sensory input without help from our surroundings. We must, of course, take our share of the responsibility and do as much as possible to alleviate the pain, but our efforts need to be met with understanding and compassion by neurotypicals.

But how do you know if the way you experience the world is abnormal? Some things to look out for is if you have meltdowns when you've had too much. Other more long-term symptoms can be exhaustion when you come home from work, or the need for longer and longer periods of recovery after being in a sensory overstimulating environment.

There's also sharp pain from things others experience as nice, or strong aversions towards different textures or touching. Frequent headaches are common, and itching or aches from seemingly minor irritations.

If you want to go through more detailed testing to see if you react more strongly to sensory input than others, you should

Google "sensory processing disorder" along with "test" or "questionnaire." This will give you a good selection of sensory sensitivity examples.

In addition to that, I've made this chapter in the book a priority, and I'll share quite detailed experiences for each of the different senses in the hope that it will help you learn about yourself.

But I don't want to only focus on how sensory sensitivity is negative. This particular part of autism can be seen as both a gift and a curse. If your dislikes are intense, it can stop you from doing things you enjoy. But if you also experience pleasurable things more intensely than others, it can give you access to types of sensory ecstasy other people will never have.

When I dislike something; it feels like pure hatred. But if I enjoy something, it feels like untainted love and passion melted into one, and it can be wonderful.

You probably also know that there are people who can see nuances that others don't register at all. And they can do great things with it.

Some autistic women are fantastic artists. Their ability to see things that work together or to hear beautiful tones can make them able to create something that other people enjoy, but aren't able to make themselves. It has for example been scientifically proven that some people on the spectrum have a superior ability to identify and remember pitch and melodies (Stanutz et al., 2012; Heaton, 2003; Bonnel et al., 2010; Jones et al., 2009).

This is true for more things than just art. If you're producing clothing or towels, and you have such a strong sense of what feels wrong to you, it can work as a motivator for you to find something better. And it can also enable you to find something that feels good. Other people can appreciate the finished product, but since they weren't that badly affected by the original version you disliked, they never thought of improving it.

To get a better understanding of your sensory experiences, you first need to know the basics. When we're kids, we're usually taught that we have five different senses. They are:
1. The visual sense, which is what we see.
2. The auditory sense, which is what we hear.
3. The gustatory sense, which is our perception of taste.
4. The olfactory sense, which is our sense of smell.
5. The tactile sense, which is what we can physically feel by touching it.

In addition to that, we have quite a few more senses depending on how detailed you want to go. In this chapter I will also mention the following:
6. The vestibular sense, which is our balance, rotation and otherwise movement in space.
7. The proprioceptive sense, which is how our joints and muscles move and which position we're in.
8. The interoceptive sense, which is what we feel inside our body.

For the remainder of this chapter, I will go through issues and advantages for each of the senses before I go deeper into what you can do if sensory sensitivity bothers you.

Auditory

Some noises can feel more intense to us than to others. This means that background noises in a café, or the sound of traffic, can be so loud that you're unable to focus on a conversation with a person right next to you. Auditory discrimination can also be difficult, which means we can't always filter out unwanted sounds.

Some autistic people also have a strong aversion to specific sounds like chewing or other bodily functions. This condition is called misophonia and is fairly common.

One thing that often triggers me during a normal day at work or out in public is the background noise. I sit in an open landscape, which is pretty bad for someone with auditory sensory disorders. I can't focus, I'll get agitated and I might end up having a meltdown or get a massive headache just from trying to get through the day. In addition to other people's voices, sudden or repetitive noises from alarms or construction bother me even more.

I properly got a taste of how painful this could be when the tenant below my office in London decided to redo their entire floor, and spent a year loudly drilling and knocking things around. It was so bad that it was impossible to shut the noise out with headphones, and we had to go out to coffee shops nearby if we wanted to take a call.

There were times during this when I couldn't go to work because it would give me too much physical pain. Several times, I had to leave while in the middle of something because it felt like my body was exploding. I think I also shouted at one of my bosses in the middle of a meltdown because of this.

For some reason, most of my colleagues were slightly annoyed, but not even close to being so negatively affected as I was. This meant that I felt I had little understanding of my need to disappear. I was even told off one day when I said I had to work from home because of the noise.

Since I didn't know at the time that I was autistic, it was difficult for me or anyone around me to understand that I could become so angry by having people drill in the floor below me.

Under normal circumstances, I solve most of my sensory issues by wearing noise-cancelling headphones at all times. This means while I work and anytime I go anywhere. If I have to travel or walk into a store, or just walk around somewhere with people or traffic, I put on a pair of headphones to play some nice music instead.

It sometimes bothers my husband if he's there because he feels like it means I don't want to talk to him. But as he begins to see that doing this helps me from having a meltdown out in public, he's also getting on board with this, and he understands my need to protect my senses.

This is harder with my friends than with my husband. The reason friends want to hang out with you, is often that they want to talk to you. And talking will be very difficult if you're always wearing headphones.

I try to put our outings to places that are less crowded or noisy so I won't be as affected. But the real trick is to have friends who get it when you need to cover up.

I'm lucky enough to have one friend who really understands and leaves me by myself in those situations. We've travelled together in the past and gone to several museums. Walking at someone else's pace and hearing all the chatter that comes with a full museum would usually be an absolute nightmare for me. But when I go somewhere with him, we just walk around at our own speed, and I listen to amazing music. One time when we were visiting a church in Rome, I had the best and most intense experience I've ever had with art. It made me so happy to realise that I could experience this and that there were ways for me to enjoy public places.

The joy of music is something that really adds to my life. I can get really caught up in it when I go to see an opera. I have some favourite songs that I play again and again, and they make me feel alive and part of something bigger.

I've had love affairs with both black metal and classical music, as I see the beauty in each of them. And I feel a physical tingling in my entire body when I listen to a song that resonates with me. It's a very pleasurable feeling, and I can see the hairs on my body move while the music plays. This isn't uncommon for people on the spectrum.

Experiencing something through another sense than intended is called synaesthesia. It means that something in your neurology makes you either join several senses, or experience input in one sense as a reaction in another. For some people, this means they can smell colours or taste words, but for me, it means I can physically feel music touch me, which isn't too far from the truth since sound waves move through us.

Several studies have shown that synaesthesia is quite common amongst autistic people. In one experiment, researchers found that out of 164 autistic adults, 18.9% experienced some form of synaesthesia while only 7.2% of the control group did the same (Baron-Cohen et al., 2013). This is similar to the 17.2% that was found in a smaller study the same year (Neufeld et al., 2013).

It has also been found that autistic people and those with synaesthesia share several aspects of their sensory experiences. When testing people with synaesthesia and people with autism together, both groups show a higher percentage of hypo- and hypersensitivity than the control groups (Ward et al., 2017).

I think that those who experience a strong degree of synaesthesia through tasting colours or seeing sounds are gifted with a very rich sensory life. And I think that to some extent, even if you're not classified as having this, you could still experiment to enrich your sensory life by combining different stimuli like listening to music while going to an art exhibit.

Visual

Visual hypersensitivity can both be about needing to avoid bright lights or feeling an attraction or aversion towards certain colours or objects. It can mean that you like looking at something and can't move away from it, or you can prefer to cover your eyes to protect them.

I find bright lights mildly annoying. When I was a child, I would always sit inside and read with the shutters down and a lamp as a light source instead. I also crave shade if I'm outside in the sun. And if I'm watching television or reading, I like the room I'm in to be lit by lamps. With too much or too little light, I get a headache.

When walking down stairs or through a small corridor, I get dizzy if the floors have extreme patterns and colours. At the same time, I can feel drawn to moving objects, and I like to follow things that move up and down with my eyes.

Other things like strong colours or specific patterns can be triggering for some people, and I think it is for me as well. I've for example had a fascination with holes since I was a child. I find them slightly disturbing, but I can't look away. I can stare at someone's pores for a very long time, as I visualise them as holes.

When I walk outside, I hate stepping in the middle of a shadow or crack in the sidewalk. I feel as I'm in some sort of imbalance, and I need to immediately correct it by stepping in a similar way with the other foot. This led me to have a very weird walking pattern as a child. I could suddenly take one short and quick step to make sure the other foot landed on a shadow. As an adult, I've learnt to relax this somewhat, but I still feel it.

Overall, I would say my visual sensory issues are few. But I frequently wear sunglasses outside, also when it's not summer, and I feel like it's a nice shield that puts something between me and the outside world. I'll sometimes keep them on when walking into a store, and it makes me feel more comfortable. It can to some come across as I'm "too cool" to take my shades off, but it's just a matter of comfort.

I believe that people with very strong visual input might be the ones who get the greatest gifts when it comes to creating art or excel in engineering. Finding specific patterns intriguing or experiencing light more intensely could lead to very interesting art choices.

Gustatory

Many children refuse to eat certain types of food because they don't like the taste. This is even more common for autistic children, and it's also normal for autistic adults.

In addition to an aversion to certain flavours, it's also normal to find different textures problematic. This can be anything from the mushy feeling of cooked mushrooms to pieces of warm apple in a pie.

As an adult, you don't need to care that much about what other people think of your eating habits. But as a child, this is different. Children are expected to eat what's put in front of them, and being a picky eater is often associated with being difficult.

And oh boy, was I that difficult child. I had huge issues with different food textures as well as trouble swallowing pills or other medication. I would frequently hide under the table to get away from it, and I would try to leave most of the food on my plate whenever I was served dinner.

Both my mother and my father would scream at me when we were sitting at the dinner table. I was threatened with all types of punishment related to food and eating. No TV if I didn't eat up, no other food that day if I didn't eat the dinner they made, and I was also frequently denied leaving the table because I couldn't eat it all.

It wasn't fun, and I felt like my relationship with my parents suffered because of it. They were of the opinion that only spoilt and uneducated children had special food, and that learning to eat new things is a part of growing up. To some extent, I agree, and I eat a lot of different things today. But only because my preferences changed when I grew older.

A basic thing that my parents never understood, was that a child who exhibits this type of behaviour isn't doing it to be difficult. In general, I believe you won't accomplish anything as a parent by making your kid eat something they clearly have difficulties with.

Being forced to eat or drink something you can't stomach makes it worse, and I think that will never be a viable option for parents who want to help their children overcome sensory sensitivities related to food. Yelling at them or punishing them because you had to eat it when you were young, won't make it easier for them.

Children aren't doing it to be difficult, and you're exposing them to physical pain in addition to the psychological stress of being yelled at or pressured. Think about the relationship you'll have with your child if she's afraid of you or have nightmares about you trying to force-feed her something that's making her physically ill. Be kinder. Your child's preferences can be a phase, or it can be long-term. Either way, you won't accomplish what you want by being a dick.

If you are the person having trouble with textures, it's important to stress that any changes or improvements must to be on your own terms. And the best way to change anything is to experiment. If your biggest issue is textures, you can try new ways of cooking to see if you're able to enjoy food you otherwise can't stand.

For example, I have an issue with most types of salads because I feel like they scratch my throat when I swallow. For cold dishes, I've discovered that I'm able to eat lamb's lettuce, which has very soft leaves. To be able to eat other types of greens, like kale, I rather make them into crispy and salty treats in the oven, or I mix them into a smoothie or soup where the texture will disappear anyways.

If you become used to new types of food, you can end up finding joy in food and cooking because you're so sensitive to new textures and tastes. Even though it might not sound believable given my limited diet as I child, I love fine dining. I'm not a great chef, but I like to think that I'm good at understanding what works well together. And with one of my autistic friends who feels the same way, I frequently taste my way through some pretty amazing combinations at the world's best restaurants. We sit together and enjoy our food and wine, often in silence, and we mostly discuss aspects that have to do with what we're currently eating and drinking.

For some people that are extremely sensitive to taste, I imagine that they can be pretty good chefs. They can taste nuances and combinations that other people don't think of, and in the same way artists can make music or pictures, great chefs can make little masterpieces on our plates.

Olfactory

Smell and taste are closely linked, so if you're very sensitive in one area, you likely struggle with the other as well. Normal dislikes for people on the spectrum can be foul body odours and industrial smells. But perfumes and flowers can also feel like torture.

I'll get a headache if I stay in a building where someone has painted earlier, or where very strong scents from cleaning are still lingering. And I can notice smells than no one else are able to identify. If there's smoke in a building down the street, or if there's been an issue in a restaurant I walk into, I'll know.

Some smells can also have an extremely positive connotation for me, and this is probably one of the reasons wine tasting is a hobby of mine. There are some really intense Champagnes that give me so much pleasure that it sends my entire body shooting through another galaxy when I smell them.

If you have a very sensitive sense of smell, I would suggest trying wine tasting to see if you like it. You can also buy aroma sets where different scents are separated so you can train yourself to recognise each of them individually. It can also be helpful for you to understand which smells you enjoy and which you resent.

Butter, petroleum and some flowers are my strongest positive triggers. But there are tons of others, and spending time with them is very enjoyable for me. And using the scents you love can help you mask the scents that bother you. Some people like bringing a scarf or a sweater with a smell they enjoy so they can cover themselves out in public should they be in a situation where they dislike the smells around them.

Some of the smells I enjoy are linked to happy childhood memories. Like freshly toasted bread with butter and milk. Or the sweet smell of Lillies of the Valley which grew near my grandmother's house.

Smells can also be very strongly linked to negative memories. This means that some scents can be a much more powerful trigger than you would normally expect. What I'm sharing next is related to what can happen when you have a traumatic memory linked to something you're already sensitive to. For the remaining part of this sub-chapter, there is a trigger warning for sexual abuse, conflict and suicide.

I've always had a very strong aversion to cigarette smoke. It is in general, a foul odour which fills your entire body with poison. It also sticks to your clothes and hair, so it will follow you around for a long time.

In an incident which I'll further elaborate in the chapter about abuse, I ended up being raped as a teenager. The man who raped me smelled extremely of cigarettes and kept breathing in my face the entire time. Ever since that episode, the smell of cigarette smoke has been able to send me back to those memories. Since I'm already sensitive to the smell and notice it when other people don't, this sensory sensitivity has given me more trouble than any other.

The story I'm about to tell is known by very few people. And it's a story I'm ashamed of because it doesn't paint me in a great light. Some might even go as far as saying I'm the abuser in this next scenario. I still want to share it because I want other people to understand how extreme sensory issues can become. And if someone on the spectrum struggles with the same at some point, I want them to know they're not alone.

I was studying in a small city in Norway and living with my boyfriend. Our apartment was in an old building without much isolation between the different units, but it was still pretty nice after we bought it and my boyfriend redecorated.

After we had lived there for a couple of years, our idyllic surroundings suddenly changed. I was studying in the living room one afternoon when I was suddenly hit by a PTSD flashback. There was smoke around me, and I desperately cracked a window open to try to figure out what was happening.

After looking everywhere for the source, I thought I had imagined the entire thing. But throughout the evening, the smoke kept coming back, and I got more and more distraught.

It turned out that the municipality had acquired the apartment below ours and moved a middle-aged woman in there. She acted odd from the beginning and I felt very uncomfortable around her. The minute she moved in, she started smoking excessively inside without opening any windows or trying to clear the air. The smoke would then quickly flow into our apartment both through the floors and the ventilation system.

I started by asking her nicely if she could use our back yard or make sure she put in proper isolation or aired her apartment when smoking. She refused. She said that she didn't care if it affected me, and that she could do whatever she wanted. I then let her know that I had a lung disease, as I had recently suffered a lung collapse and spent quite a lot of time in the hospital. One of the risk factors is smoke, so I was also extremely worried about my lungs collapsing again. She still refused and slammed the door in my face.

This kept going on for months. She would smoke excessively every day, and I would get so affected I had to leave the apartment, but only after going downstairs and yelling at her through her door. It only took seconds from her lighting up until I could feel my eyes and nose burning and all I could think about was being held down and forced to have intercourse with a man three times my age. With the added anxiety coming from the risk of suffering another lung collapse, I turned into a completely different person those months.

I physically couldn't get myself to stay inside when she lit up her cigarettes. I was wandering the rainy streets of the city at 3 AM to avoid the smoke when I was supposed to be up studying for exams the next morning. I was crying and shaking and didn't know what to do.

We had long screaming matches in the hallway, and I called her the most horrible names I've ever called anyone. In a desperate effort to try to drive her out of the building, I started playing black metal extremely loudly so she would understand how it felt getting your personal space invaded. But that only resulted in the other neighbours complaining about me.

She seemed to get some kind of thrill out of torturing me, and I went into something that can only be described as the barest minimum of human functioning. It was so intense and lasted for so long it has all turned into fog in my mind. With no support from my boyfriend or neighbours, I started considering taking my own life.

Instead, I managed to get my boyfriend to contact the municipality who owned the flat, and they eventually agreed to look for another place for her. However, this didn't happen quickly, and our confrontations became more and more aggressive.

She started posting notes in the hallway about what a despicable human being I was. That I was ruining her life by getting her kicked out or her flat. I responded by telling her how pathetic she was. And then one day she stopped. The smoke disappeared as well. For nearly two beautiful summer months, I could live peacefully at my own place again. Until another smell started taking over. The sweet smell of rotten flesh filled the hallways.

Since I had worked at a hospital as a teenager and frequently been down at the morgue, I recognised the smell of death. My boyfriend called the police, and they came to remove her body. We were never told what had actually happened, but I assume it was suicide.

I couldn't help but feel relieved. The sense of being free again overpowered what should have been sorrow and regret for this person who had clearly been suffering. And a small part of me was also happy that it hadn't been me.

People I've told this to have judged me. And I get it. In retrospect, I should have shared my concerns more calmly with my boyfriend and made him fight the battle for me in a more humane way. If I would have had this diagnosis at the time, it would have probably helped as well, as I would have been better at understanding and subsequently explaining why her cigarette smoke drove me into such a craze.

This story can seem irrelevant and boring, but I want you to understand how deep sensory issues can run. Not just because we're more sensitive to the smells, tastes and lights around us, but because we can also be additionally triggered by the memories our senses are holding onto.

Tactile

Tactile oversensitivity is easy to understand because it's how we react to physically touching something. And it's what you'll most often see examples of when you read about people on the spectrum. Issues with tactile sensitivity are also often easier to do something about.

It can be clothes that don't fit properly or labels that gnaw their way into our skin. Socks with their unforgiving seams are also popular hate objects for children and adults alike.

For as long as I can remember, my one mortal enemy has been dry cotton towels. My gym has horrible towels and trying to lift one off the shelf is a nightmare every day. As long as I don't have to touch them with my fingers, I'm usually fine, and I've developed a weird technique where I lift them using the sides of my hands and elbows.

I also don't like to see towels close to me, so I try to keep them out of the bedroom or other places they might have been used. When I see my partner use one, I feel unwell. If I think about towels or talk about them, all the hairs on my body stand up. If I've just cut my nails, it gets worse and there's no way I can touch one the rest of that day. One of my greatest fears is to have someone force me to put a towel in my mouth. I feel ill as

I'm typing these words, and I need to breathe and try to think of something else.

The same goes for fabrics like corduroy and some types of linen if it's mixed with the wrong materials. As with my food, I have huge issues with some types of textures. But I don't hate everything I touch, and I've also realised there are a few weird things I can't get enough of.

My parents often had to pull me out of the grocery store where I was found sitting in a corner caressing a sack of flour or rice. I would also stick my hand inside packets of flour whenever my mother was baking. The nice velvety texture against my skin was so nice. And today I like all kinds of soft things that I can drag across my skin or that I can completely cover myself in.

If you're only affected by things like fabrics, I think you can pretty easily make adjustments by finding a substitute product you like to touch instead. For example, I try to find very soft towels, and if I'm visiting someone I know have bad taste int towels, I sometimes bring my own. Or I do my weird drying dance where I try to pick up the towel without using my hands. I've also dried my hands in my own hair on more than one occasion.

But tactile sensitivity doesn't only cover things that we touch. We will also often have issues with the way other people approach and touch us. For example when someone puts their hand on our shoulder and we hastily shrug it off because it tickles us. Autistic women (and men) are notorious for disliking soft touches. While deep pressure and body contact can be sources of soothing sensations, most soft touches that aren't initiated by us feel painful and intrusive.

Issues with being touched by others can greatly impact our relationships with people we're close with. It can for example be the relationships between parents and kids when an autistic child refuses to be held or cuddled. The parents might describe how their child will start screaming or trying to run away when they approach them to show affection. Or even violently protesting a loving hug.

When we get older and try to build romantic relationships, it can get even harder. It can be difficult to be intimate with someone if we can't stand the way our partner touches us. Something that's supposed to be the ultimate display of affection, can instead drive a wedge between you and your significant other.

When the sensory sensitivity is coming from the way someone else touches you, it's also more difficult to make adjustments. Are you supposed to ask them not to touch you at all, or do you need to control the way they act when they're near you? It can be hard to get that message across without hurting anyone.

My first encounter with the dislike of being touched by others came in first grade. All the students were expected to line up outside the school entrance and hold each other's hands. The girl I was paired with had tiny, pointy and dry fingers. The feeling of her pressing her hand into mine made me shiver, and I got in trouble with several teachers for refusing to touch her.

As an adult, you wouldn't be forced to hold someone's hand, but there are several other situations where you're expected to be physically close to another person. When there's an issue, you should try to be sensitive about it because this is an area where people are easily hurt when you criticise them.

I've had to explain to all the people I've dated that they need to lay off my knees and navel. Some people think it's fun to challenge it, but it's not funny anymore when my reflex is to kick them as soon as I feel anything close to my knee.

If you're dating an autistic woman, I would advise you to take it very seriously when she tells you about something like that. It's not to be difficult, and if you ignore our warnings, it will seem like you're trying to take our bodily autonomy away, which isn't a good feeling for anyone.

But if you are the person who is affected by tactile sensitivity, you should focus on the ways you enjoy being touched by your partner. I love getting deep massages, and I like to feel the weight of someone on top of me. Make sure your partner understands what you like and ask them to read up on sensory sensitivity if they don't take you seriously to begin with.

When you encounter people you don't know very well, the only thing that's efficient is to get away from the situation. I hate crowds where people brush into me; or full buses where someone's leg is suddenly next to mine. In those situations, I'll just leave without any explanation. I've found that nothing good comes from trying to educate a stranger.

In general, you should try to surround yourself with all the things you like to touch. Build your bed into a sanctuary that you love to spend time in. Buy clothes that feel right for you. And feel free to buy other sensory toys that feel good for example by tickling your skin.

If you don't find a product that feels the way you want it to, there's nothing that says you can't be the person who makes it. If you really dislike something because of how it feels, I imagine there are other people out there who do too. Your sensitivity puts you in a unique position when it comes to making a better product. I thought about making and selling a softer towel and launching it on Kickstarter, but when I checked, this had already been done by several teams before me, so it seems I wasn't the only one with the idea.

Use your sensitivity to make things comfortable for you, and see if you can use any of your experience to help others.

Vestibular, proprioceptive and interoceptive

This part of the sensory system is what people are usually baffled by when they hear about it for the first time. Because most of us learnt that our body only has five different senses when we were kids. I think there's an argument to be made that some of these senses are part of the tactile sense, but for the sake of sensitivity, I'll discuss them separately.

Your vestibular sense can best be understood as anything that affects your balance. Some people are prone to getting car sick for example. I can get that at times as well, but mostly I love things that affect this sense. I love spinning in my office chair or laying in a hammock or a waterbed. It all feels great, and I crave it as often as possible.

That's the thing with sensory sensitivity. Sometimes we want less of something, and other times we crave more. You need to figure out what you like and make sure you allow yourself to do the things that feel good.

The proprioceptive sense is the feeling of where your body parts are moving. If you struggle with this, you can suffer from poor coordination skills since it will be hard for your brain to know exactly what each of your body parts is doing.

My hand-eye coordination is ok, and I'm a decent tennis player, but I still struggle to eat without spilling food. And walking down the stairs can be challenging because I often feel like I don't know exactly where my legs are.

Finally, the interoceptive sense is our internal regulation. It's our feeling of what's happening inside our bodies and sometimes also what our bodies are telling us to do. This means that you can be over- or under- sensitive to your body's signalling when it tells you that you should use the bathroom.

And I think we all know what happens if you can't read those signals. Not being able to properly read signals for hunger and thirst can also be a big problem. If you struggle with that, you should definitely set up a reminder system so you don't go an entire day without eating or drinking, and potentially also discuss it with a doctor.

What you should do if you want to improve sensory issues

Although sensory dysfunction is a separate diagnosis, it's also seen as a part of autism in the DSM-5 criteria. Since sensory issues are a part of the diagnostic criteria, we can assume that a large part of the autistic population is affected by this, but I don't know exactly how many. Some researchers have tried to estimate this, but what I've been able to find is diverging both in their definitions of what constitutes sensory issues and how they're measured, meaning the results are all over the place. Some researchers are also citing non-existing numbers, making it even more difficult to find trusted reports on the topic.

In the beginning of a meta-study on the effects of sensory interventions for children (Case-Smith et al., 2015), the researchers state that 80% of children with autism struggle with co-occurring sensory issues. However, when I read through the original report that was cited, which is called "A Meta-Analysis of Sensory Modulation Symptoms in Individuals with Autism Spectrum Disorders" (Ben-Sasson et al., 2008), it doesn't ever give an estimate of the percentage of children on the autism spectrum that struggle with sensory dysfunction. And the only time the number 80% is used in the report, is when the researchers label groups of children with more than 80% autistic participants.

It makes me question the researchers' ability to properly

read and understand studies when this is, in fact, the first sentence of their report. I tried contacting some of the authors to get them to clarify where they got their numbers from, but I was unable to get a response from any of them.

Overall, I need to say that I'm severely disappointed by the quality of research done on sensory sensitivity. And I struggle to understand why it's so hard to stick to rigorous statistical methods as well as properly reading and understanding the content of other studies before citing them in your own research. When we try to figure out what can best help us with sensory sensitivity, it's important to be able to rely on research. Without it, we can end up wasting both time and money on methods that are proven to be completely useless.

I'll try to summarise the most important things I've found from going through available research. But the first thing you need to do if you have issues with sensory sensitivity is to map out what you struggle with and what sensory input you enjoy. It's difficult to try to improve something if you don't know how you are affected. I've included this mapping as a part of the next self-work section.

You can also get help from a professional. While you might already work with a talking therapist, occupational therapists are usually the ones who specialises in sensory problems. You should try to seek out an occupational therapist who has specialised in treating people with autism or sensory processing disorders.

Most interventions and treatments for sensory dysfunction is based on getting adequate sensory input to help us regulate ourselves. This can for example be done by setting up sensory diets. This diet is usually an hourly schedule of different activities you need to do so you get input to the different senses on a regular basis. This can be done by swinging, carrying heavy objects, eating or chewing on specific textures, training or other things individually tailored to your sensory needs.

One other popular technique often included in a sensory diet is the Wilbarger protocol. The protocol requires you to use a specific type of brush on your arms, legs, back and feet to give deep pressure followed by manipulating your joints. This is done every 90 to 120 minutes for a couple of weeks to give the optimal effect.

It can sound illogical that you'll be better able to handle sensory input by giving the body even more to process, but I do see that some types of input can be calming whilst others are distressing. As an example from earlier, I hate light touches, but I love lying in a hammock swinging back and forth, and I can experience a calming effect from the latter. However, I have struggled to find research that properly documents the effect of this.

In Sharon Heller's (2014) book "Too Loud, Too Bright, Too Fast, Too Tight," she shares several encouraging examples of people who experienced great results from implementing sensory diets and brushing using the Wilbarger protocol. However, I miss references to studies showing the effects of these treatments in larger samples.

When searching for them, I mostly find smaller pilot studies for adults showing positive effects of the treatments, but without larger randomised studies, it's hard to conclude that they will definitely be worth the effort.

There are more studies available on children, but none of them meet the standards one usually expects to see in the medical community. In an effort to do a systematic review of all research done on the Wilbarger protocol on kids, researchers were only able to find four studies that were peer-reviewed and otherwise matched the criteria of looking exclusively at applying this protocol (Weeks et al., 2012). All four studies had extremely few participants, and none of them included girls. In total, there were only eight children across all four studies. This means there was no testing against control groups, which is a fundamental part of testing the effect of almost anything. Further, the studies lacked descriptions of how well the protocol was followed, and before and after measurements seemed more arbitrary than anything else.

Some of the effects were interesting and worth mentioning here. For example did one study look at spit-measured cortisol levels before and after the Wilbarger protocol was applied. Here, the cortisol levels of the boys either decreased from high to medium or increased from low to medium, showing that the protocol's effect was to get the cortisol levels back to a more "neutral" level (Kimball et al., 2007). However, when no control group is available, one can't assume that the effect comes from applying the protocol only, and it might as well be a natural mean-reversion which would have occurred without any type of intervention.

This was also complicated further by the way the testing was set up. Cortisol levels were measured in two saliva samples, one before and one after the protocol was applied. But the boys were set to do 15 minutes of "quiet neutral activities" between applying the protocol and taking the second saliva sample, which means that the change in cortisol levels could simply come from this and not from the brushing itself.

Another systematic review of sensory interventions for autistic children found some positive effects from the different treatments, but not enough to draw any conclusions (Case-Smith et al., 2015). I'm a bit reluctant to cite this study, as this is the same as mentioned earlier which was using incorrect data in the introduction of the paper, but I'll still go through the major findings.

The researchers looked at two different types of interventions. One was done in a clinic and directed by an adult, and the other was supposed to be done by the children themselves in their normal daily environments. The first method showed some positive effects, but for the second method, there was no evidence of improvement. The second method included several studies done with weighted vests, which had little to no effect on the children wearing them. And the one thing most of the studies reviewed had in common was great deficiencies in research methods. Most of them lacked control groups, weren't randomised, had a limited number of participants, methods for recruiting participants were inadequate and there was bias introduced because observers were the ones reporting how the children felt.

It's important to note that a lack of larger studies following rigorous research criteria doesn't mean that the treatments don't have any effect. It only means that there isn't sufficient evidence to prove it at the moment.

If I consider my own experiences, I can easily understand that deep pressure, swinging or exercising can have a calming effect on the nervous system, as these are things I crave myself to able to relax.

And no matter what the available research says, you should take your sensory limitations seriously. It's not just to get over something and toughen up. Sensory overload can harm you both mentally and physically, and you can expect to feel exhausted if you don't take care of yourself in those situations. Some sensory issues can be outgrown as we get older, but they might never disappear completely.

Self-work

The best way to start is to try to identify which sensory input that bother you and what you find pleasant. You can use this as a starting point when speaking with an occupational therapist, or you can work on building a sensory kit for yourself.

A sensory kit is something you can bring with you when you go out so you can cover up anything that bothers you. A standard kit consists of headphones with access to music you like, sunglasses to protect your eyes from harsh light, and a pleasantly smelling scarf to cover your mouth and nose.

Below, I give an example of how you can fill out a form for each of your senses. I've used my own experiences below so you can see different types of examples. If you want a printable sheet to work on, you can go to my website (christinelion.com) and download a pdf.

1. Auditory/Hearing

Dislike: People talking in the background, the sound of someone chewing, children crying, drilling or other maintenance work, sudden and loud noises, dragging furniture across the floor.

Like: Very loud music, running water, listening to the same thing over and over again.

2. Visual

Dislike: Very strong light, a dark room if I'm watching a screen, patterned carpets on floors and stairs.

Like: Same colour in several nuances, same colour on several things for example with matching sets, small holes.

3. Gustatory

Dislike: Big mushrooms, any type of cooked fruit (for example apples in apple pie), berries or chunks in jam, diced tomatoes from a can, the inner part of large tomatoes, large pieces of sushi, green bananas, yolks of hard-boiled eggs, large pills, all types of liquid medication.

Like: Rice cakes that have laid out in the air for a day so they're really dry, pasta that has cooled down and laid outside so that it's stiff and cold, melted cheese, glass or other surfaces I can chew on.

4. Olfactory

Dislike: Cigarette smoke, smoke in general, other people's sweat or body odour, strong scents from washing or paint.

Like: Butter, toast and brioche (especially in wine but also if someone is making a toast with butter), chlorine, petroleum, coconut, lilacs, jasmine, really intense and rich champagne right after the glass has been poured.

5. Tactile

Dislike: Dry towels, corduroy, stiff clothes or fabrics, dry skin, light touching or stroking on my skin, pressing on my nails, touching my knees in any way, touching navel, touching at all if I'm tired.

Like: Rice and flour, either alone or inside bags where I can press them into shapes, soft fabrics or tassels I can drag across my skin, a fly walking on my arm, deep pressure massage.

6. Vestibular/Proprioception/Interoceptive

Dislike: Sudden movements.

Like: Spinning, sitting in a rocking chair, lying in a hammock, being in a waterbed, floating in water.

Stimming

Why and how we stim

Stimming, or self-stimulatory behaviour, comes as a natural continuation from the previous chapter. Since women on the spectrum suffer from issues with sensory input, we can also have very strong sensory needs that we satisfy in untraditional ways. Often, these are some of the first things parents notice about their autistic children.

Kids often seem to enjoy a lot of movement. They like being rocked, spinning around themselves, flapping with their hands, or sometimes even hitting their head against something hard.

When I was a kid, I had several "bad habits" as my parents liked to call them. It seemed to be impossible for me to stop biting my nails, cracking my knuckles, saying the letter "s" softly, spin around, rock back and forth on a chair, or play with any soft fabric I could find. I also enjoyed chewing on glass, which ended pretty badly on more than one occasion as my parents had to pluck tiny pieces of broken glass out of my mouth. But chewing on it felt so soothing and nice.

My mother thought most of my sensory habits were unnecessary, annoying and would hurt my ability to develop proper social connections since many people don't find stimming socially acceptable. "If you don't stop that immediately, no one will like you and you won't have any friends in school," my mother often yelled at me when I was doing something she found annoying.

But I couldn't stop. I didn't do it to be mean or to annoy the people around me. Stopping would take all the willpower I had and then some. I spent so much time planning and writing lists as a kid. If I just managed to stop biting my nails. If I could only stop making those noises. Then people would like me, and I would be perfect.

My mother thought I was careless and didn't bother to pay attention to her frequent reminders to stop twitching and twirling. But the truth is, I made great efforts trying to stop annoying her. But it was so hard, and I didn't understand why. Eventually, I started believing that I was just lazy or bad at behaving out in public.

But those activities aren't just annoying habits for kids that don't know better. They're actual sensory needs that must be satisfied. When someone is stimming, they're doing it because they enjoy the sensation it brings, and not because they're trying to annoy other people. Although it's unclear exactly how it works, it seems to stimulate the nervous system and helps us make sense of things.

We use stimming in several types of situations. We can be anxious, in an overstimulating environment, trying to distract ourselves from something else or just feeling the need to get stimulation in an area that's under-stimulated.

Stimming can be almost anything that gives input to the sensory system. Some common activities amongst children are flapping the hands, swaying back and forth, rocking, staring at lights or things that move, saying the same words over and over again, making a particular noise, rubbing the skin, scratching, biting, grimacing or smelling something.

Many autistic adults still enjoy some of these things, and I bought a rocking chair when I turned 30 that I use it all the time. I also like spinning on office chairs or using a swing if I find one.

But when I first read about stimming in a book about autism, I automatically thought it was something I had never done as an adult. Then I started recognising some of the little habits that help me get through the day.

It turns out I never got rid of my habits after all; I just replaced them with other types of behaviour. This is something I've discovered is typical for women on the spectrum. They learn to either hide it or take on more socially acceptable behaviours. As we start to decode what's socially acceptable or not, we begin masking our stimming. It doesn't mean we stop doing it, but it becomes less visible.

Today, I don't bite my fingernails, but I bite and flick on the skin next to the nails, almost always until it starts to bleed. I also bite the inside of my cheeks and my lips, play with my hair, bite on pens, or I spin in my office chair.

In addition to the behaviours above, which I've learnt are quite typical for autistic women, I also have a few behaviours at home that my husband has to live with. I repetitively watch the same films or series again and again. I prefer watching a movie I enjoy 50 times instead of watching 50 new ones. It's soothing, and I like knowing how it ends. I also like to keep films playing in the background while I do other things. I've even broken several computers in the bathroom because I like to watch films while I'm washing my hair.

In some situations, we want to change or in some way redirect our stimming. Some behaviours are frowned upon in public, and some can also be harmful. But it's important to not suppress our natural need for sensory input just because we don't want to come across as weird. Doing that can be harmful to our health and wellbeing in the long run.

As I mentioned earlier, many autistic women become masters of masking their symptoms by swapping one stimming behaviour for another. This can be done on purpose or just happen naturally because the surroundings keep giving them negative feedback.

Some behaviours that can be seen as more socially acceptable are playing with a fidget toy while working or focussing, and if you're out in public you can keep it in your pocket and play with it out of sight. Also, behaviours that act like grooming are more common for women out in public. This can be fixing your hair, makeup or nails.

If you keep doing any of these things, you might think that you're not dependent on stimming, but you are. And if you spend time every day trying to stop yourself from doing something that feels natural, it's probably time to figure out a way to give yourself a proper outlet for whatever your body needs.

There are sensory toys you can buy that are specifically made for stimulating autistic kids, but they can also be great for adults. Fidget toys that can spin, twirl or jump are tempting for many of us. There's also jewellery that's made to be chewed on, and there are soft fabrics we can play with. A search on Amazon or eBay for fidget toys or autism toys will give you plenty to choose from. Take a look around and see if there's anything you feel that you need.

I've bought a little rubber ball made of hundreds of threads. It bounces up and down and feels really good to squeeze. I keep it in my office for when I'm really stressed or to distract my body while I'm stuck on long calls. At first, I thought my colleagues would stare at me when I was throwing my ball around, but it turned out they were as intrigued with it as I was, and now there's more of us playing with little string balls when we're on the phone.

Needing something to stimulate our senses when we're stressed or having to force ourselves to be still for long amounts of time seems to be almost universal. So it's not just autistic people who will enjoy stimulating their senses, but we probably need it more often.

Don't be embarrassed by the things you need to do. Instead, make sure you're aware of the situations when you need stim. Intentionally putting out things to touch and play with can help improve your focus. And let's face it, it's also a lot more fun than sitting still on a chair.

Self-work

Write down what you've previously considered to be habits of touching things or moving around to see if they can be considered stimming. It can help to think about things you do with each part of your body, and then about what you do in stressful situations during the day.

Take the things you identified and think about what sensory need you're trying to fulfil by doing those activities. Decide if it's a habit that bothers you, or accept that this is something you need and are fine with keeping in your life. If you're doing things that are harming you, like excessive scratching, try to find other inputs you can use to satisfy the same need. Start on the top on work your way down:

<u>Finding your stims:</u>

1. Do you scratch your scalp or bite and pull your hair?
2. Do you bite your lips, cheeks, pens, drinking bottles or other things that feel good to chew on?
3. Do you frequently touch your face?
4. Do you crack your knuckles?
5. Do you constantly pluck your hair?
6. Do you fidget or move your fingers around repetitively?
7. Do you spin on your chair or push yourself back and forward?
8. Do you flap your hands?
9. Do you tighten your muscles until they cramp?
10. Do you bite your nails or peel off skin?
11. Do you "mindlessly" eat chips, nuts or other things that are crunchy?
12. Do you feel the need to squeeze things really hard or put heavy things on top of you?
13. Do you jump up and down or sway side to side when you're standing?
14. Is there anything you do repetitively in front of the mirror in the morning when you're getting ready?
15. What do you eat each morning?
16. Is there anything you start doing if you're on public transport and your surroundings are overwhelming you?
17. What do you do when you're in at work and are trying to concentrate?
18. Are there any objects you carry with you everywhere or that you touch when you don't need to?
19. What do you do when you're trying to fall asleep at night?
20. Do you move around or touch things while you're on a call?

Executive functioning

Leading a mini-company

Executive functioning sounds like an elusive concept, but it's actually a way of describing something very practical. It captures all the little things you need to manage your life and make it run smoothly. Exactly the same as an executive officer would do to run a company. It includes planning, setting goals, organising, being flexible, having a good working memory and impulse control.

There seems to be a general consensus that people with autism do worse on these things than neurotypicals. And from a medical perspective, issues with executive functioning can come from damage to the frontal lobe, or from several neurodevelopment disorders (Hill, 2006).

A meta-study going through research published on executive functioning from 1980 to 2016 showed that autistic people performed worse overall than neurotypicals (Demetriou et al., 2018). However, there are some reasons to believe that these results aren't accurate for the total autistic population. The same study showed that the reported differences were decreasing in newer research. This could be because many of the people who were diagnosed with autism as early as the 1980s were also suffering from learning or intellectual disabilities, meaning this could impact the result (Demetriou et al., 2018).

Since several of the tests for executive functioning are based on asking participants to solve puzzles, sort cards or other things that can frequently be affected by the participant's IQ, it seems like this could be a part of the effect they're picking up. From what I've noticed in some of the older studies, the autistic participants have been matched with neurotypical children solely based on their age, and not age and IQ which is typical now. This means that the people tested might not have struggled with the tasks only because they were autistic, but because they also had learning or intellectual disabilities.

It also seems that when comparing studies on self-reported and measured executive functioning, autistic people experience themselves as worse than they actually are (Demetriou et al., 2018). This is good news for us since it means we probably perform better than we think. Hopefully, it's not the result of poorly designed tests.

Another positive thing to note is that the differences between autistic people and neurotypicals are larger for kids than for adults. This could be the result of improvements as we grow older and learn to use coping mechanisms to help us in the areas where we are weak (Demetriou et al., 2018). With this in mind, it should be possible for us to improve if we find appropriate techniques tailored to our issues.

And improving is key when it comes to these topics. Executive dysfunction is obviously an issue where just embracing our differences will not provide the best results. If you keep losing things or forgetting to file your tax returns, it will have negative consequences for you. This is why this chapter will spend more time than elsewhere on addressing each issue and what you can do to improve. Some of the tips and methods I've had good results with myself, and some I've gotten recommended from other people on the spectrum.

Losing your things

This first part is one of my least favourite categories, namely losing your things once they're out of sight. When the nice and eccentric math professor goes looking for his glasses and everyone can see that they're already on his head, it's charming and cute. But if you're the person who has to look for her phone, keys, glasses or credit cards several times a day, it starts getting annoying. And other people don't find it charming when they have to wait for you to go to back to a restaurant for the third time that week because you have no idea where your keys are.

I can't count the times I've lost my debit or credit card and had to register all my payment details with Amazon, the gym, Apple pay and everything else I depend on to function. I also have at least one mini panic attack each day when I have to look through my purse for my phone or my keys.

They're usually there, or I'm able to retrace my steps to find them. But it makes me feel bad; as if I'm constantly failing at something everyone else can do perfectly fine.

Therefore, losing things is something I've tried avoiding for a long time, and I have a couple of tips that can be helpful. The first is an annoying recommendation that my friends always have given me: Find a specific place for each of the items you frequently lose.

Since I often lose my keys, I got a glass box and put it right next to the entrance. All the little things that go in and out of my bag end up in that glass box when I come home. I put keys, wallet and sunglasses there. Since it's easy to see through the glass box, I'll always notice if my things aren't in it.

Complement this with a rule saying that you should always check your pockets before you take your jacket off and that you should take out the keys and wallet and put them in their special place whenever you get home. I also have a rule saying that I don't put a bag in my closet without emptying it. This means I sometimes have a lot of bags lying around, but at least I know which bags to check if I'm missing something.

I've also started to keep other things in boxes around the apartment. Since each thing gets a "home," I know where to look for it, and it makes it easier to have a system. Just make sure that when you place something in a new place, the placement is logical so you can deduce where it is if you don't remember right away.

To stop losing your cards, you can try going online instead. If you live in a country where Apple pay exists, you can use this instead of your card. If your card doesn't leave the wallet or your house, it's less likely to be forgotten somewhere. For those horrible times when you still lose your card, I find it helpful to have an additional card and a separate account so you can transfer money to the other card and use this as a reserve when you're waiting for a new one. You can also use this card when you register memberships etc., or you can set up a direct debit on your account instead of using the card. This works with Paypal, electricity, water companies and several of your other utilities. That way you don't have to go to all your service providers and give them your new card details every time one disappears.

Avoiding to lose your phone can be difficult since most

people bring them everywhere they go. This is why I've found it to be more efficient to streamline the process of locating the phone again. You can always ask someone else to call it, but that won't work if you're alone, or if your phone is in silent mode. My solution for this has been an Apple watch. It has a button you can click that makes your phone send out a loud beep. I use it several times a day, and I didn't even think about how useful it was until I had to send the watch for a repair. Suddenly I had to spend time looking for my phone again.

I realise that getting an Apple watch is a very expensive solution, but there are other similar things you can do to make finding your phone and other items easier. Several companies sell small bluetooth trackers you can put inside bags or hang on keys that will make a noise when you ask them to.

Keeping it clean

Cleaning skills aren't frequently mentioned in studies on executive dysfunction, but since it demands skills in planning, memory and flexibility, I find it fair to include.

Some autistic people are super good at cleaning, but many of us are also incredibly messy. I know because I'm one of them. As a student, I've lived in apartments where I didn't clean for months at a time, and I think I vacuumed once the first year I went to university. Everything was lying on the floor, and it was a horrible mess. For some reason, I also didn't understand that it would be embarrassing if other people were visiting and saw all of it. Luckily, I learnt later when living with a very clean boyfriend that it isn't socially acceptable to have people over when your place is dirty.

When I moved away from this boyfriend, I went through a long process where I realised that I had to learn how to clean properly. The first step was to accept that being able to clean an apartment and keeping it tidy isn't an ability everyone is born with. It's something that has to be learnt, and it is possible.

Like many before me, I learn a lot from reading "The Life-Changing Magic of Tidying Up" by Marie Kondo (2014). Yes, it's a bit quirky as it asks you to go through everything you own and throw away anything that doesn't spark joy, but it has several useful tips. The author is very good at describing her systems for sorting, folding clothes and keeping an overall clean environment. I used it to rearrange all my closets, and now five years later, I still use her folding method whenever I put clothes away.

There are also ways we can force ourselves to stay clean by using our other strengths. If it's one thing autistic people are good at, it's creating systems and rules. So use this to your advantage. One of my rules to help me keep things clean is to ask myself one simple question every time I finish an activity. "If not now, then when?" Unless I can see a good reason why I need to put it away at a different time, I have to do it right away. And if it needs to be done later, it has to go in the calendar so I know when it's planned. It makes it hard to find excuses to put things off. I mean, do you want to include cleaning up those dirty dishes in your calendar or do you want to do it now instead?

Another rule that works well for me is to bring something with me every time I go from one room to another. Before I started doing that, my rule was that if I thought I had to carry something from that spot sometime next week, it wasn't worth picking it up now. Trust me, you don't want that to be the rule you follow since you'll end up living in complete chaos.

To get laundry done easily, you can buy one of the laundry baskets with four separate rooms and sort your clothes when you take them off in the evening. That way, washing your clothes seems like a much less daunting task than if you have to sort a mountain of laundry before you can put anything in the machine.

If I follow all of these rules, I'm able to keep the mess to a minimum. I still don't love to do anything that has to do with cleaning, so I also hire help. I have a cleaner coming in once a week so I never have to vacuum or wash my floors. If you can afford it and you struggle with cleaning, I would recommend doing this. When I was a student, this was financially out of reach for me, so I know it's possible to do it alone, but I prefer to get help when that's available to me.

If you can't afford to pay someone every week, it can be helpful to have a friend be there with you when you start doing the initial decluttering. Getting it clean in the first place can be a very intimidating task, and with someone else around, it's harder to slip away and do something else.

Personal hygiene and clothing

Keeping up with personal hygiene and making clothing choices are other things many autistic women struggle with. I thought it was surprising to read at first, and I didn't want to think of myself as within that category since having poor hygiene comes with such a stigma. It's something you would expect from someone who has completely lost it or someone who doesn't have access to a home with a shower etc.

However, since many autistic women have issues with executive functioning, they also tend to forget some of the routines that others take for granted. Especially if we don't see a logical reason why we should keep up with them. And showering can easily be forgotten when you're busy reading about your special interest.

When I was a kid. I didn't care at all about my personal

hygiene or clothing. If no one told me to brush my hair or clean my teeth, I wouldn't have done it. I would also walk around in a sweater with food stains if my mother hadn't prevented me from it.

As an adult, it's much more subtle. I don't wear dirty clothes on purpose, and I have a routine for showering, brushing my teeth, and doing my hair and makeup every day. But if the routine is disturbed, I can miss out on all of it. If I go to bed too late and I'm too tired, I can skip brushing my teeth or taking my makeup off. If I don't go to the gym, I can go a few days without showering before I notice that I need to do it.

One of the reasons I've been able to improve in this area is that fashion and makeup started to become a special interest of mine after I turned 20. I had long-term projects where I learnt one thing at a time for personal grooming and became completely obsessed with it. It took me several years to learn how to make intricate eyeshadow patterns, fix my hair, wear heels, do my nails and buy necklaces.

If doing hair and makeup interests you, I'm sure you will be able to do the same. But if you don't have any wish to conform to society's beauty standards for women, there's nothing that says you have to do it.

I feel like it's important to clarify that it isn't necessary to spend time becoming good with makeup, shoes or clothes if you don't want to. There's no rule saying that women have to look a certain way or use makeup and heels. The most important is to make sure you keep yourself clean so it doesn't affect your health.

But if you're at the stage where you want to keep up appearances to a certain extent without putting too much effort into it, I can share the few things I did to simplify these routines for myself.

For fashion, especially at work, there are a few easy rules

you can follow. Get help from someone or make the effort yourself to build a small capsule wardrobe. This means that you make sure that most of your clothes fit together, and finding something that works each day will be less difficult. Choose one or two dark colours for bottoms and two matching colours for tops. Then buy all of your clothes in those colours. Super easy, and no one will ever notice that you're not putting any effort or imagination into it.

One superpower that I use to trick myself into being better at personal care is that I love sets of matching colours. It's a weird thing I have, but when something comes in similar colours and clearly belongs with something else, I love using all of it. I just wish my favourite skincare products came with a matching toothpaste and toothbrush.

Paying bills, filling out forms or opening letters

Another executive skill that all adults need to master is administrative work. In your personal life, this is doing things like paying bills, opening letters, filling out tax forms or setting up insurance. For some of us, this feels overwhelming.

I'm bad at it myself, and especially if I'm busy. One embarrassing and pretty horrible moment for me was when the tax authorities decided to go through my taxes several years back in time. My taxes were all done correctly, but they had asked for more information to document costs related to the sale of a property. It wasn't during the time of year when we usually do our taxes, and I was super busy travelling at work. This meant I didn't look into it for several months. When I did, it turned out the deadline for providing the supporting information had passed. I called a lawyer and had him help me file the paperwork, but it was still too late. They redid my taxes and claimed a pretty large amount paid in. Not only did they do that, but they took more than three times what they claimed that I owed them and also sent a letter to my employer saying they would take my salary directly from them.

It was horrible and embarrassing, and it took me six months and one lawsuit to get my money back. At the time, I was working for a large Swedish investment bank, and my hours were crazy. I sometimes slept in the office and spent more than 100 hours a week working. Self-care and personal administration went right out the window, and I never spent any time at home. In a situation like that, I'm sure a neurotypical would have struggled as well, but maybe they would have been quicker at reacting when something first went wrong.

Since this experience was so unpleasant, I've tried putting systems in place for catching similar issues early. I have deadlines in my calendar for when taxes should be filed, and for unpredicted events like this, I put it in my calendar to read through mail or log onto government systems to see if everything is as it should be. If I see something that I know I can't deal with it at the moment, I put it in my calendar for the weekend to make sure I don't miss anything.

For bills, you can set up a direct debit, which usually works, and getting help from someone you live with to read through mail on a regular basis is also useful. As a general rule, I've tried to accept the fact that administrative tasks aren't something we can do once and then be done with them. It's something we need to do most days for the rest of our lives, and there's no way around it.

For many of the quirks autistic women have, I can usually find something positive in it as well. Not for this one though. Missing out on deadlines only have bad things associated with it, and if I could change this about myself, I would do it in a second. It's annoying and time-consuming when something goes wrong, and being able to plan and execute is a core part of being in a functioning family as well as society.

I'm really good at doing it for my job, and much of my day-to-day work is execution related, but putting the same effort into my personal life just seems like a struggle. I'm currently trying to analyse all the things I'm doing right at work to see how I can apply those same efforts at home, and hopefully, I'll have something to share with others once that's done.

Memory

Women on the spectrum tend to have an uneven memory profile. In particular, some of us struggle with short-term memory and the context of things we're supposed to remember.

In one study, autistic adults with normal IQs were tested against a similar sample of neurotypicals. The tests for short-term recollection of words and numbers showed that there were no differences in the amount of information that could be recalled between the two groups. But when the information had to be recalled in the correct order, autistic people struggled more than neurotypicals. This led the researchers to believe that people on the spectrum have trouble remembering things in the appropriate context (Poirier et al., 2012).

For long-term memory, it seems to be more difficult to find good studies. But some meta-studies mention that there are overall fewer differences between autistic people and neurotypicals here. And for some types of memorisation, autistic people actually outperform neurotypicals. For example, rote memory, which basically means to learn by repetition, seems to be better in autistic people (Goh & Peterson, 2012).

I've always thought it was weird that I can solve almost any mathematical problem as long as I can doodle on a piece of paper in front of me, but when someone asks me a simple arithmetic question and wants me to solve it in my head, I'm lost. I bombed my dream job interview with one of the biggest private equity firms in the world because I completely froze when I was asked to do some quick calculations with a share price. Give me a problem that's ten times harder when I sit alone with a piece of paper and I'm ok. If I combine my poor working memory with having to do it in front of someone when I'm nervous, my brain will turn to mush.

My short-term memory isn't good, which is probably also why I keep losing things. But I'm lucky enough to have an extremely well-functioning long-term memory. For school, work or most other pursuits in life, that type of memory can come in handy. When I studied, I was always able to read for memory-based exams for a short amount of time and still get a 6 or an A. By visualising pictures, I can memorise absolutely anything. If you struggle with your long-term memory, I suggest you read up on the mnemonic technique called "method of loci" to get a proper description of how it works.

I also remember many conversations word for word, and my childhood memories extend back to before I turned two, which is extremely early. I've seen it mentioned several places that autistic people tend to remember things from an earlier age than what's normal because we can use our strong sensory inputs for recollection. It's an intriguing thought, but I haven't been able to find any studies that prove it, so it's probably just a happy coincidence that I feel like my memory works that way.

Functioning labels

Poor executive functioning skills can make life very difficult, as we usually have to manage administrative parts of our lives continuously. And I know that several autistic people, myself included, struggle with the things I've been through in this chapter.

Yet, many of us are still labelled so-called "high-functioning." We're supposed to not need help because we have high IQs and no learning disabilities. But does that really mean we're better at executive tasks than people who are considered "low-functioning"?

One study that tested more than 2000 children under the age of 18 diagnosed with autism showed that IQ was a fairly weak predictor for how they were functioning in everyday life. This can lead us to believe that the term "high-functioning autism" is wrong, as even people without learning disabilities will report that they struggle in their personal lives (Alvarez, 2019). This is also one of the reasons why most autistic people don't support the use of functioning labels. Autism is a spectrum of uneven abilities, and being "good" at one thing, doesn't mean you're better at everything else as well.

In addition, it's something of a derogatory term, as if we're not individual human beings with our own opinions, thoughts and needs. When I've told doctors about my diagnosis, some of them have asked me "but you're high-functioning?" And most of all I want to reply "Yes, I am. Are you?" Until we also start lumping neurotypicals together in groups of high- or low-functioning, I'm not sure it makes sense to do that to autistic people.

Self-work

The self-work in this chapter will be about figuring out

which rules you can use to make your personal life easier. The rules can be related to cleaning, self-care, paperwork or bills. Try to make your rules logical. If you don't think the logic behind them makes sense, this isn't likely to give you any positive results. Use the list below to help you get started.

Make rules and cues to get your life on track:

1. Throw out all things you don't need anymore, as they will be in the way and create unnecessary chaos for you.
2. If you need help, reach out to a friend or a cleaning company to help you get started with a foundation.
3. Make a set of rules that tell you when and how you should clean specific items. For example dishes every time you eat or laundry every time you change your sheets.
4. Go through the tax reporting for the country you live in and put all important dates into your calendar, including when you need to start to work on applications or filling out forms. Do the same for other things you need to fill out regularly, like insurance paperwork.
5. Make a routine for opening letters the same time each week and set up standing orders for bills you need to pay monthly.
6. Find a spot for the things you often lose or get a device that can track them.
7. Come up with routines for mornings and evenings to get all your self-care routines done. Writing down each step is helpful.
8. If you struggle to start a task, try a thought exercise where you write down what is stopping you from doing it, and write out how it would go if that thing was removed.
9. Decide on one important thing you need to do each day,

and do that first.
10. Sometimes, working during unexpected hours of the day can trick your brain into doing things quicker. I'll be super slow if I try to put my clothes away in the evening, but if I do it in the morning when I have to get to work, I'll be extremely efficient. A tiny bit of pressure works.

Special interests

Intense knowledge

    Having so-called "limited interests" is a part of the DSM-5 diagnostic criteria, and it has been observed all the way back from when Asperger started studying children on the spectrum.

    Some people find it annoying when an autistic person starts telling them all the details of their special interests, but I find it fascinating. It means that we're extremely passionate about a few things that properly interest us, and I would never consider that to be negative. The deep and detailed knowledge can be very impressive, and very close to what we should consider a superpower.

    And most of us have a special interest. One study which was done predominantly on autistic boys in pre-school and elementary school showed that 75% of the youngest children and 88% of the older children had a special interest (Klin et al.,

2007).

It doesn't mean that neurotypicals don't also have hobbies and interests, but they're not as invested in them as autistic people are. In fact, just by knowing how intense someone's special interests are, researchers have been able to predict if they're on the spectrum 77.5% of the time (Anthony et al., 2013).

When the same study tried to compare which topics autistic people were interested in, there seemed to be quite a lot of overlap with what neurotypicals were interested in. However, there was a statistically significant difference when it came to interests related to facts and attachment to objects (Anthony et al., 2013). This is consistent with the findings in the first study, where young autistic boys often were interested in fact-finding and learning (Klin et al., 2007).

As you already know, it's a problem that most studies on autistic people have been done on boys. That's the case for both studies I've referred to on special interest as well. This means we don't have proper knowledge about girls' special interests.

Why does this matter? Because it's not given that women and girls have the same interests as boys. This can make it more difficult for parents or teachers to recognise early signs of autism in girls. If they aren't into the stereotypical trains or car brands, they're more frequently overlooked.

It doesn't mean that girls and women can't also like those things, but they're also more likely to have interests that include movies, famous singers or even reading fiction, which is something we often assume autistic people don't enjoy.

It's also a misconception that the special interests have to stay the same someone's entire lives. Special interests can be lifelong and follow someone from they're kids until the day they die. They can also be short-lived and intense.

Because of all of this, some women don't realise they have special interests. They will read about almost any subject, but since it's not the same subject all the time, it's hard for them to understand that this is their special interest. They can also have one interest following them their entire lives, but since it's not something we usually connect with autistic interests, they still won't consider it a special interest.

Another thing that's also often overlooked as a special interest is attachment to objects. If you think back on what you were doing as a kid, you probably had some toys that you loved more than anything else. Those toys could have been the first signs you were showing of having a special interest.

As a kid, I had a tiny and soft toy monkey and rabbit that I got as gifts from relatives. I took them with me everywhere I went, and I couldn't stand seeing anyone else touch them. I was so attached to them that my parents had to steal them out of my arms while I was sleeping so they could wash them.

When I grew older, I threw myself into books. Reading and learning have been my longest and most intense interests. I learned to read before I started school, and it was my favourite activity. I would re-read "The Secret Garden" in bed at night, trying to hide my reading light from my parents. During warm and long summer days, I would go inside and pull the shutters in front of the windows so I could read in peace. And in school, I would much rather spend time with a good book instead of being with my classmates outside.

If the teacher talked about Nietzsche, Kafka, Joyce or Dante as footnotes in our literary history, I would go to the library and take them all home with me. Reading led me to writing, and I wrote several novels in my teens and early twenties. One was even picked up by a publisher, but I abandoned my dream of becoming a published fiction writer when I realised how much of the text my publisher wanted to change.

But in addition to reading, I also had other weird interests as a child. At around seven or eight years old, I developed an interest in real estate ads. I was reading them intensely, and I even wrote songs and poems about the properties I liked the most.

In retrospect, I think my primary motivation for taking up such an intense interest in real estate ads was motivated by feeling like I didn't fit in where I grew up. I thought that by changing my surroundings, I could change who I was and the way other people saw me. I had always felt like an outsider, both with peers and with my family, so I was creating my own little fantasy world in each of these houses where I was normal and people liked me.

This leads me to think about the reasons people on the spectrum develop such intense interests. I think it can be a way to escape a reality where we don't feel comfortable. With our interests, we can build something else that isn't connected to the people around us or to the reality we feel so alienated from at times.

Another theory about special interests is that since autistic people don't enjoy spending time socialising, they need to find something else to do in their free time. That seems overly condescending, but maybe it has some truth to it.

An explanation I find more compelling is that we need something that will help us relax and decompress after spending time around other people, and that our special interests make us do that.

I've had periods where I spent all my time working with absolutely no time to do anything else. It made me feel like I was surrounded by chaos. And I couldn't think clearly until I was back to reading, writing or spending time with one of my other interests. Doing that calms us down and makes us feel like there's order in the world.

Special interests can also be a source of social interaction and friends for us. If you find someone else with the same interests as you, it means you have something to connect over. Not only can this be the start of a new friendship; it can also be the start of a love interest or a lifelong partnership.

So it's clear that our special interests have some kind of function to us. Not only can they be useful in their own right; they can also help us in other areas of our lives. They could for example be used as motivation to finish another task you struggle with. They can also be incorporated into learning so a child will pay more attention since it's related to something they already enjoy.

For others, the intensity of their special interests can become a problem. Mostly because they take over for everything else in their lives. They forget to eat and refuse to do homework because they would much rather read the latest book on their favourite subjects. It can also become a financial issue for someone who spends all their money on buying books or model trains when they should pay their electricity bill instead.

And I can surely understand how special interests can become overpowering. When I start with something, I can't stop. I need to learn absolutely everything about it, and it gives me such joy and meaning that there's nothing else I would rather spend my time on. I'll easily turn down dinner invitations with people I normally enjoy spending time with if I'm exploring a special interest. Showering or going outside have also gotten second place more than once.

But these issues are few, and I see more sunshine stories than anything else. Special interests can even turn into extremely successful careers. Consider some of the high performers in certain types of industries. I bet quite a lot of them are on the spectrum. Not only are they bringing an intense and unbreakable focus to their jobs, but they're also approaching the subjects from a different point of view. And they do it with a passion never seen before. The results can be astonishing.

I even think that our special interests are the closest we have to actual superpowers. Combining our ability to hyperfocus, our attention to detail, and our tendency to pick an interest and stick with it can make us unbeatable. But I won't start speculating here about which famous people within tech, acting, writing or other areas are on the spectrum.

We should remember to celebrate our special interests. Becoming an expert on something can be extremely valuable when we need to earn a living. And don't be ashamed by your special interest no matter how nerdy or weird it is. We should be proud of what we can learn and achieve. And although we probably need to understand when other people are bored when we talk about our special interests, we shouldn't need to hide it from the world. The passion you have is unique, and you need to take care of it.

Self-work

The exercises in this chapter will be to map out all the interests you've had in your life and looking at how they can be helpful for you now. If you're going through the process of getting an official diagnosis, this list can be helpful to show your therapist as well, as he or she is likely to ask you about them.

Map out your special interests:
1. Start with your childhood. Were you extremely attached to any toys or other objects?
2. Did you collect anything?
3. Were there topics you kept talking about to adults or other children?
4. What did you like to read about?
5. What do you do in your spare time today?

6. Do you do any activities that feel particularly relaxing for you?
7. Do you have deep knowledge of things that others don't?
8. Are there people who could benefit from learning from you?
9. Do you have ideas on improving products or creating something from one of your interests?
10. Are there things you have trouble finishing that you could use your special interests as motivation for?

Controlling your emotions

The Empathy Quotient

I've already mentioned that it's widely believed people with autism have low empathy. But is there any truth to that?

To start digging into that question, we first need to understand what empathy is. There are several definitions, but they all revolve around having an appropriate emotional response when you recognise someone else's feelings or situation.

It's important to note that empathy isn't the same as sympathy, and many people actually mean sympathy when they say empathy. While someone who has empathy recognises a feeling in someone else, someone who has sympathy wants to do something to help a person who needs it. So even if an autistic person has less empathy than a neurotypical because they struggle to recognise someone's feelings, they could still show more sympathy by wanting or trying to help.

Several researchers have tried to compare the empathy level of autistic people and neurotypicals. But it's very difficult to do that without also assuming that the person being tested has the same knowledge of social conventions as the people who set up the test in the first place. Since we don't know exactly what empathy is and how it works, it's also difficult to measure.

Simon Baron-Cohen has together with autism researcher Sally Wheelwright tried to find a measurement scale for empathy. They named it the Empathy Quotient (EQ), and it consists of 60 questions of which 40 focusses on empathy and 20 are there to confuse the test subject (Baron-Cohen & Wheelwright, 2004).

To see how their questionnaire worked with autistic people, they set up a pilot study consisting of 90 people with an autism/Asperger's diagnosis and 90 age- and sex-matched neurotypicals. They all had IQs within a normal range.

While 81.1% of the autistic people scored less than 30 points on the test, only 12.2% of the neurotypicals did the same (Baron-Cohen & Wheelwright, 2004). To understand what this means in practice, we need to look closely at the type of questions used in the test.

Some of the questions were related to knowing how other people feel, and others were about rudeness, hurtful remarks or lying to give someone a compliment. These are not necessarily the things people think about when discussing empathy, and it's problematic that the definition is set by a neurotypical standard.

We have different values than neurotypicals. We are more honest, and we care about facts. It doesn't mean that we don't care about people and want the best for them, but we wouldn't lie to make that happen. If someone becomes upset because of something you say, does that mean you're the one who's wrong and the person with the hurt feelings is right?

There were only two questions where the group of autistic people scored higher than the neurotypicals. One was about being late to meet a friend, so if empathy was more about being truthful and respectful of other people's time, autistic people would definitely come out on top of this test.

When Baron-Cohen and Wheelwright did clinical interviews with autistic people to ask them about their EQ scores, they all reflected on the fact that they had no intention of hurting someone's feelings. If it was pointed out to them that something was hurtful, they felt bad about causing pain for someone else. Which brings us back to the point that an autistic person doesn't need to be less sympathetic because they score lower on an empathy test.

When I tested myself, I scored 17 points which is within what you could expect from someone with autism. But I don't think that what I answered on those questions accurately describes my ability to feel bad for other people, it just means that I care more about being truthful than anything else.

I know several women on the spectrum who have a lot of sympathy, and I do too. I care about animals, nature and other people as well, but I admit I find it hard to feel sympathy for someone who has put themselves in a difficult situation. For example did I reply "strongly agree" to the statement "it is hard for me to see why some things upset people so much." It doesn't mean I don't understand that people are upset if someone hurt them or they suffer from a disease. But I don't see how people get upset when someone else tells them that what they said was wrong. Does it make me less empathic? According to this definition it does, but it doesn't mean I'm any less likely to care for someone who suffers.

In fact, I believe that since we've usually struggled a lot in our lives, we can be very understanding. And I think we have many things to offer someone emotionally because of this. Who is more capable of feeling sorry for someone who feels left alone or alienated than someone who has suffered from those exact same things themselves?

One of the things I was afraid of when I was younger was that I lacked empathy or sympathy and that this meant that I didn't care about others. But I know now that I care strongly about how other people are doing; it just presents itself in a different way. In fact, I would argue that both I and other women on the spectrum can be extremely sensitive. Sometimes we struggle to understand what other people are feeling, but we're always ready to help when we see that someone suffers.

Recognising your own emotions

For too long the world has believed that people on the spectrum lack the ability to feel anything for others. But some people go even further and claim that an autistic person lacks the ability to feel themselves. Hence, they think that it's impossible to hurt our feelings because we don't have any.

As I'm sure you know, we can easily get hurt, and many of us know that all too well after trying to find our way in a sometimes unforgiving neurotypical world. But we're not always good at recognising nuances of the feelings we're having. And some of us have trouble both understanding and describing our emotions.

One study tried to explore autistic people's ability to be self-aware. This was done by testing for something called the self-reference effect. The effect describes a bias commonly seen in neurotypicals, and it makes them good at remembering words that have been used to describe themselves. While no improved memory is showed when words have been used to describe others.

The group of autistic people who were tested showed the same tendency, but not to the same extent that the neurotypicals did. At the same time, the autistic group scored higher on a self-reported test for Alexithymia (Lombardo et al., 2007).

Alexithymia is a condition where a person is unable to identify and describe their emotions properly. It's more common amongst autistic people than neurotypicals, but can be both temporary or a trait you're born with. Even though this is a separate condition from autism, it's still a part of the symptoms many autistic people show without having received a specific diagnosis for this.

It can be frustrating when you're not able to tell your feelings apart, and it can isolate you from others. It can also be difficult to know what you want, or to stand up for yourself, if you're not entirely sure of what you're feeling.

I know that I frequently mistake other feelings for hunger, which is one of the reasons I struggled with eating disorders as a teenager. I also have trouble recognising nuances of irritation, disappointment and anger, and I frequently lump everything into the anger bucket, which makes me react accordingly.

Showing anger when what you're really feeling is hurt isn't necessarily a good thing. If a date cancels something you had planned and you feel hurt because you're not being prioritised, picking a fight isn't likely to get you much sympathy. But if you admit that you feel hurt, you might get an explanation and some comforting without ending up having a huge fight. I've made the mistake of attacking someone I care about when what I really wanted was reassurance many times in the past. And it has never gotten me anywhere good.

Much of the reason for this has been that I was never in touch with my feelings. And I never took the time to explore that I could be vulnerable since I thought that would make me seem weak. But ignoring my feelings didn't make me strong; it made me unhappy and confused.

If you can understand what you're feeling, you're closer to communicating it to people around you. And this again will lead to more appropriate reactions from others. But the most important part is that you're more likely to show yourself more sympathy and compassion if you acknowledge what you feel.

At the end of this chapter, I'll introduce some exercises you can use to start identifying and describing feelings, and I hope you'll spend some time doing that. But first, I want to go through some other issues we often have when it comes to showing our emotions.

Not showing happy emotions

Another part of being autistic that certainly doesn't help is the lack of facial expression. Often, our faces are in a neutral to negative fold, and we tend to not put on a wide smile even when we're happy.

It doesn't mean we don't have feelings, or that we don't want to share them with others from time to time. But we might show them in a less obvious way, and our faces don't always match our emotional state.

As you're probably aware, society in general tends to be increasingly annoyed with women who don't smile or show "appropriate" emotions. I would say that this isn't our problem, but it still affects us. Other people can view us as negative or emotionless and treat us differently because of it.

I was working at my first job when my boss put a name to the phenomenon: resting bitch face. It wasn't new that people around me thought I was angry or sad when I wasn't. And I frequently got negative reactions because of it. My mother would yell at me for looking mad when I was sitting somewhere by myself because it annoyed her. Her favourite expression was that I looked like I had "seven sorrows and seven worries on my shoulders." Other people regularly asked me if I was sad or if anything was wrong. And even in kindergarten, I was often told I couldn't leave the table until I smiled at one of the adults.

It got increasingly frustrating because I didn't understand how my face could look so uninviting. I found that one thing I could do was to look at myself in pictures and see if I was happy with what I saw, or if I thought that I needed to change my facial expression.

I used to hate posing for photos. It didn't matter what I did or if I had gotten dressed up in advance. My pictures always came out horrible, and I couldn't understand that the person looking back at me was the same I encountered in the mirror each morning.

In my late 20s, I decided to make an effort at learning how to pose in front of a camera. It started with selfies, then I had my boyfriend take pictures of me. I treated it as any other special interest and read blogs and watched videos of how to place my body. And after a while, I was able to look closer to how I felt. I also accepted the fact that no one looks good all the time.

This sounds like a very superficial thing to do, but it did give me a better understanding of myself. It helped me to see for the first time, that yes, I can look like I'm pissed off when I want to look like I'm happy. And it also made me aware of the fact that I look even sadder because I hunch my shoulders and look down on the ground all the time.

I'm not saying that anyone owes a smile to anyone else, and if that's not how you're feeling, you shouldn't be pressured into it. Doing that is a form of masking, which we have already established is unhealthy. I'm the first person to get annoyed when women are asked to smile so they can seem more attractive. All I'm saying is that if you want to become better at showing your emotions to the world, there are ways to do that.

But I would still never be comfortable carrying all my emotions on the outside. By nature, I'm not someone who will show excessive joy or enthusiasm by jumping up and down or yelling.

Sometimes it has been an issue with people I've been close to because they didn't feel I was sufficiently sharing their happiness or showing that I enjoyed what we were doing. I haven't been able to change that. It simply doesn't come naturally to me.

Another reason why women on the spectrum often can be viewed as negative is that we tend to make comments on small things that are out of place. That excellent attention to detail along with our sensory sensitivity will make sure we always know if something isn't working the way it should.

We think that we're only stating a fact. Maybe we're describing how something can be improved, or we need to process all the sensory input around us by talking about it. But we don't intend to be negative. I rarely think "oh, now I'm going to rain on your parade and make your day miserable."

Most of the time, I don't even understand that what I've said is seen as a negative comment by others. In fact, it can be very hurtful when people say that I bring the mood in a group down, or that I'm constantly negative and difficult to be around. It certainly isn't a compliment, and when you don't understand that you're doing it, it can be hard.

It's always a good idea to try to explain your thought process to the people close to you. Then they will hopefully respect that this is part of who you are and that they shouldn't read anything else into what you say. Neurotypicals have a tendency to believe that any negative comment about something you're doing with them can be interpreted as criticism of them personally. They're weird that way, but since they lack our ability to be straightforward, they often fall for emotional traps like these.

If that doesn't help and you really want to make other people comfortable, you might need to start identifying when you make negative comments and keep them to yourself. You can write your thoughts down, or you can try to say it in a different way. If you at the same time acknowledge something nice about the person or their efforts, it's usually received a lot better.

But most of you shouldn't do that. If we're not always being uplifting and cheerful, it doesn't matter. What's best for our health is to be true to ourselves and not pretend to be someone else. If we truly are unhappy, and we want to change that, it's a completely different thing, and should be dealt with in another way.

Depressed by society

We've already explored that some autistic people have a tendency to look like they're angry or depressed. But are we actually more frequently troubled by depression and anxiety? Unfortunately, the answer is a clear "yes."

Estimated numbers of how common depression is amongst people on the spectrum wary a lot. But depression and anxiety seem to be some of the most common psychiatric disorders that appear together with autism (Stewart et al., 2006). This adds to the issues already faced by us, and depression can be difficult to battle in addition to other problems.

One sad truth is that some women probably are depressed because of the backlash they face from other people due to their autism. Many studies show that women are more frequently punished for not following social norms around them, which can make it harder for women on the spectrum to be accepted by a group.

We know that women who show behaviour that's atypical for their gender are judged as less socially skilled than men (Rudman & Glick, 2001). And when they succeed in tasks that are traditionally viewed as typically "male" they're not only deemed less competent, but they're also considered to be a lot less likeable (Heilman et al., 2004). Women are supposed to be good at "the social stuff" and hence will face a greater negative reaction when they don't meet that expectation.

Not understanding yourself and not fitting in isn't a recipe for bliss and happiness in a world where social skills are so highly valued. Women who aren't diagnosed might even suffer more because they have no explanation for why they feel like they don't fit in with other people.

As you can see, depression amongst autistic women is a complicated issue. And we can't know for sure if autism in itself gives a higher probability for depression, or if it's the treatment people on the spectrum receive from society that makes us more prone to suffering from mental health issues.

But it should be enough for us to know that we need to do something about it. And what does it cost to be more accepting of the autistic people in your life?

Meltdowns and shutdowns

Since we struggle to understand our feelings and show them to others, one would think that women on the spectrum are always cool and in control. But we can often be accused of being very dramatic. Sometimes that's only because we're very passionate about our interests, or because we have a strong sense of right and wrong. But it can also be because we tend to suffer from emotional outbursts when we're overwhelmed.

When our stress levels have reached a certain threshold, we can end up in a state of meltdown or shutdown. Neither is defined in strict terms, but the expressions are supposed to be somewhat self-explanatory. A meltdown can consist of someone being angry, crying, self-harming, throwing things and in general losing control of themselves. In a shutdown, the person withdraws from the rest of the world and isn't able to communicate.

One isn't better than the other. They're both caused by too much stress or too many things going on at the same time, and a meltdown can turn into a shutdown. And if it does, although it might seem like the person has calmed down, it doesn't mean that the emotional stress they're feeling has passed.

It can often be very small things that drive us over the edge and push us into a state of meltdown. But that doesn't mean that those little things were the only contributions to the stress we experienced. Stress and tension can often build up over days or weeks until we finally break down.

Meltdowns and shutdowns are often associated with children on the spectrum. A young child is "throwing a tantrum" while frustrated parents and baffled bystanders are unaware of what's going on. It's considered a nuisance when this happens with a child, but when an adult does the same, most people think it's completely unacceptable. Therefore, those who suffer from it as adults can bear a lot of shame. It can be difficult to explain to those around you, and it can make you feel small and visibly different.

When people talk about meltdowns, these are the things I associate with them: complete loss of control and a feeling of eternal rage. I sometimes end up crying uncontrollably if the situation is ongoing for a long time, and I can eventually end up in a shutdown, where I go mute and leave the physical world behind. I've struggled with it since I was a child, and it's been an issue in several of my adult relationships.

But that doesn't mean that I was aware that I was having something called a meltdown. I just thought I had anger issues. And identifying a meltdown can be difficult if you don't know what to look for.

Why is it important to know that something is a meltdown and not just regular anger? Well, there can be other things you can do to ease the episodes. And sometimes it also helps to know that it's not "you" that is causing them, and that you don't have to take such a big part of the blame.

When you know that your episodes of emotional outburst are meltdowns, you can use this to identify their cause. There probably will be certain things that trigger your meltdowns again and again, and removing or reducing your exposure to them can help immensely.

One thing many women on the spectrum struggle with is overload from sensory input. Several things can be the final trigger to push you over the edge, but it has often started with sensory overload long before that happened. Too bright lights, ongoing noise or people bumping into you. This makes you much more sensitive to other things that bother you, and the reaction is much stronger than it would be otherwise.

The other triggers can be many. It can be an unexpected change in routines. It can be someone breaking a rule, treating you unfairly or talking to you in a demeaning manner. Another popular trigger is if something doesn't make sense logically and we're still forced to do it.

But for me, it's never one thing alone that pushes me into a meltdown. There are several things happening at once, and to discover what they are, you start at the meltdown and work your way backwards until you have a good overview of what happened.

I'm going to share a few examples of meltdowns that have been triggered by seemingly small incidents so you can see what I mean.

My husband and I usually play tennis on the weekend. One morning we were going to play, he said he wasn't feeling up for it because his shoulder was hurting. I was annoyed and tried to talk him into coming. I couldn't convince him to join me, but I didn't want to cancel my plans, so I still went there and spent an hour practising serving alone. On the court next to me, a woman was playing with her boyfriend. After a while, I noticed that I kept getting fewer and fewer balls and that she was playing with some of mine. I told her she had taken my balls and asked to get them back. She refused and claimed they were hers. I kept watching her and saw her picking up even more of my balls. This time I told her it didn't even make sense for her to pick up the wrong balls as we were playing with two different brands, so I could clearly see which ones were mine. She still kept lying to me, saying she had exactly as many balls as when she came in. At the end of the session, she had left behind several old, fluffy and useless balls on her court, and left with my new ones.

I was furious and called my husband asking if he could walk down to the court and come and meet me. I told him what had happened and that I was close to going off on this horrible woman. He dismissed me, laughed and said it wasn't worth getting angry about a few tennis balls since I could just go and buy new ones. Of course, I knew I could get new balls. But the anger I felt from someone stealing them right in front of me and then lying about it wasn't going to stop.

When something like that happens, the anger consumes me. It feels warm and heavy in my chest. All my muscles tense up, and my breathing becomes shallow. Often, it becomes difficult to speak in coherent sentences. Something in the back of my head is stopping me from talking properly. And all I want is to unleash that powerful demon inside of me onto whomever I feel is responsible for angering me in the first place.

When I got home, I got into a fight with my husband because he thought I was overreacting, and I ended up exploding. I got so angry I couldn't breathe. I started crying uncontrollably, and for almost an hour, all I could do was sitting on the floor and holding my legs tight into my chest. I felt pathetic. Who lets a petty thief get to her like that?

I shared the incident at an autism forum for women, and I was overwhelmed by the support. The other women told me they would have felt the same if someone took something from them, and that it didn't matter that it was something very small. They also shared bits of humour about painting big penises on my tennis balls the next time so no one would want to steal them. I felt lighter immediately. Being understood by someone can make all the difference in the world.

But you can see from this example that I was already stressed and annoyed because my husband cancelled our plans, which made it even harder for me to cope with something unplanned happening.

As I already mentioned, sensory issues that build up in the background will also often be the reason that I ultimately can't take anymore. This is why most of my meltdowns happen when I'm travelling.

The stress of being in new places filled with people, and the sensory overload from all the sounds and lights, especially at airports and train stations, are exhausting. If you pair this with schedules that are changed because of delays and difficulty getting food regularly, you have the perfect recipe for disaster.

Around a year ago, I was at the airport in Berlin with my husband when we ended up waiting in line for the passport control for 30 minutes. I felt super uncomfortable, and right before it was our turn, the officer decided that he was going to go on an hour-long lunch break. He tells the entire line that he's closing up, and that anyone who wanted to enter needed to go to a different counter and stand in line there. I got furious and wanted to hit something. Getting in the back of another line again sounded horrible, and the lack of respect he was showing the people who had been waiting triggered me on so many levels.

I marched over to the new line and even walked in front of some people that had been standing behind me in the previous queue. I was about to explode all the way through security but worked hard at holding it in. When I came to the other side, it turned out there was nothing I could buy to eat, meaning I would have to suffer through hunger for the rest of the evening. That's when I had enough and started to loudly tell my husband how this was the most pathetic excuse of an airport I had ever seen, and that the people working there should be fired if they couldn't understand the basics of operating a line. I was very loud in a very small place, which embarrassed him a lot. When he asked me to take it easy, I got even angrier, because I knew I was right. It wasn't until I had sat alone with my music for 20 minutes or so that I eventually calmed down. And I still didn't want to talk about it.

I travel frequently for work, and there's nothing that gets to me so much as people working in airports who want to enforce arbitrary and made-up rules just because they think they can get away with it. I've been angry at so many people at check-ins and controls when they claim that the rules of showing ID have changed from five minutes ago, or even more annoying things. I can't help but talk back and tell them that what they're saying is inconsistent with official rules and also doesn't make sense. They never take it lightly, and I'm sure someday I'll get kicked off a flight.

Fighting the anger monster

So what can we do to avoid meltdowns? I have a few theories that relate to the beginning of this chapter about acknowledging feelings as they happen and not letting them build up into something bigger.

One example I think illustrates this was when a boyfriend had invited me to come with him to see his family for the first time. Not only had I looked forward to the trip, but also what this meant for our relationship. But when the day of the trip came closer, he told me something didn't work out with the schedule, and it would be complicated and expensive for me to come with him. I was super disappointed, but I didn't acknowledge it at the time. I didn't say anything to him, and I ended up exploding with rage a couple of days later when I was exhausted after dental surgery.

What probably would have helped was to acknowledge the disappointment and tell him right away that the change in plans hurt me. And also that I was worried if it meant he wasn't taking our relationship seriously. I'm not saying I should have accused him of having other intentions by not bringing me, but simply stating that I was disappointed because I had looked forward to the trip and also to take our relationship in that direction.

By doing that, I might have avoided yelling at him on the phone several days later. With my current husband, this is something I try to follow as a rule. If he's doing something that makes me sad, or that hurts me in any way, I'll share it with him right away and try to discuss why it happened and how we can avoid it in the future. As a result, we've had much fewer incidents where I keep something inside for weeks and then explode over something that seems insignificant.

Talking about meltdowns and why they happen will also be very helpful for your friends and family so they can understand what's happening to you. You can let them know if there's anything they can do to help you as the meltdowns happen, but if you prefer them to leave you alone for a while, that's ok to tell them as well.

What I've told my husband is that he needs to help me *before* a meltdown happens. I can sense when it's getting too much, and I try to give my him early warning signs. I might be snappy, but I need him to understand that when I tell him not to touch me and leave me alone, it's serious. If he continues to approach me, it will only get much worse. If I'm bothered by the environment we're in, I need him to accept that we sometimes have to leave quickly.

All of these things should be talked through when everyone is calm, and not during a meltdown or an argument. In addition to talking to your loved ones, you can make an effort to minimise the things that trigger you.

Getting help to tackle sensory issues is also something that can be useful long-term. Understanding when you need to take a break is a key factor. If you tell people close to you that you'll shut down when you have too many sensory inputs at once, it can be easy to tell them you need to slip out for a while to collect yourself. Sometimes, you even need to say that you have to go home.

It can also be worth looking into your general stress levels and figure out if there are things you can do to improve your overall health situation. As I'll go more into in the next chapter, I've found meditation to be helpful. Not only can it reduce symptoms of anxiety and depression, but it could also help with anger.

Another great tip I've found to work well for myself is to

approach the meltdowns with simple and clear logic. Tony Attwood thinks that this approach can be very effective for people on the spectrum who experiences anger. We often get mad when something isn't working the way it should, meaning we have a problem on our hands. But if we get angry, our ability to solve the problem is reduced, as we're not as capable of working through anything when we get agitated (Attwood, 2006).

On the positive side, Attwood also notes that even though people on the spectrum can have what seems to be a very dramatic reaction to small things, he has seen that we can keep calm during emergency situations where other people typically panic (Attwood, 2006).

I know it can be frustrating for someone to live with our shutdowns and meltdowns, but it's our body's way of telling us we need to step back and take a break. It's a very sharp and clear message that we need to take seriously.

I don't think we should look at this as something that's solely negative. Our bodies are telling us what we should have less or more of, so we should try to understand what's behind our meltdowns.

It can also be a sign of our great need for justice and fairness. Some of my meltdowns are triggered by things I perceive to be unfair, and I would think that's an admirable quality to have, and not something to be ashamed of.

Self-work

The exercises in this chapter are divided into two parts. The first relates to identifying and describing your feelings. This will also be helpful for the second part where you'll try to identify the steps that lead you to a meltdown.

For each feeling below, try to describe:
1. What situations make you feel like this?
2. How is your posture when you get this feeling?
3. Where in the body is the feeling located?
4. What will your face look like?
5. What physical sensations do you get in your body?
1. Is it light, warm, tight?
2. Do you feel any symptoms like change in heart rate or temperature?
3. Is it more or less difficult to talk?
4. Are other bodily functions affected, ie. do you need to go to the bathroom more often?
5. Do you get a headache?
6. Do you cry?
7. Does your body go stiff, or will you shake?

Anger:
Irritated, enraged, annoyed, frustrated, mad, hostile, provoked, indignant

Anxiety:
Nervous, scared, stressed, worried, dread, surprised, concerned, doubtful, embarrassed, sceptical

Happiness:
Joyful, confident, cheerful, content, satisfied, pleased, excited, thankful, lucky, delighted, playful, thrilled, calm, inspired

Jealousy:
Bitter, spiteful, envious, contempt

Sadness:
Depressed, disappointed, discouraged, hurt, guilty, lonely, shame, grief, despair, emptiness, down, miserable, humiliated, heartbroken, desperate

Love:
Affectionate, attached, close, compassionate, desire, lust, fondness, tenderness, sympathetic, sensitive, passionate, comforted

Identifying your meltdown triggers:

For exercise number two, I want you to find some concrete examples of meltdowns or shutdowns you've experienced. Start by describing what you felt in the moment. Then describe what was happening around you. Try to trace your steps backwards. What happened right before the meltdown? What were you doing in the minutes and hours before? How did you feel that morning when you woke up? What type of environment did you spend your day in? Had anything happened with other people or places earlier that week? Try to go as far back as you can to understand if there was anything leading up to the moment where you broke down.

Once you have described a few incidents, try to see if there are any common triggers. Was there a specific person that kept pushing you? Sensory inputs that got too much? Places that didn't make you feel good?

Taking care of your health

Why we need to take particular care of our physical health

Autistic people often struggle fitting in with neurotypicals. We also have a hard time dealing with sensory issues, and we have emotional meltdowns frequently. But in addition to those things, we have a higher likelihood of several diseases and disorders. Sometimes it can feel like we've been dealt a shitty hand in life and that the world is unfair. To some extent, that's true, but there are several things we can do to improve our health if we know the risks we're exposed to.

There is a multitude of things we often forget to think about which can affect our physical and mental health. And since we're already struggling with so much in our lives, we have much less room for mistakes than the average neurotypical person. In fact, studies show that autistic people have an increased probability of premature death caused by a range of both psychiatric and physical conditions (Hirvikovski et al., 2016).

This is why I think it's extra important that someone on the spectrum learns about how to eat right, train and sleep. Giving the right input to the mind and body can put us in a much better position both physically and mentally.

Everyone probably learnt some of the basic health knowledge in school. But a lot of the things we learnt are either wrong, outdated, or not that relevant for someone with autism. Since we're more prone to getting other physical and mental illnesses on average, it's so much more important that we get to know the details.

Most of us don't understand how much we can improve our health by tweaking a few habits. And we also don't realise how quickly our health can deteriorate if we do the wrong things. That's why I hope you take this chapter seriously, and that you look into my sources and other books on the subjects if you feel like I don't properly explain everything here. Being able to manoeuvre your way through all these challenges will get you into a much stronger position to deal with everything else life will throw at you.

Comorbidities

That something is comorbid means that two or more medical conditions frequently occur together. It doesn't mean that everyone who has one disease has the other and vice versa. But it does mean that amongst the people having one of the diseases, there's a higher percentage with the other disease than in the general population.

Often, it's not known why the conditions are co-occurring. One can cause the other, or they can both have the same cause. Some diseases can also have partially overlapping symptoms. For example can anxiety and autism have several things in common. And since anxiety is often a part of what autistic people struggle with, some of us will also be diagnosed with a specific anxiety disorder.

It's important to take these conditions seriously since they can have a great impact on your day-to-day life. I think that one reason for being diagnosed with autism is to see it in relation to other things you struggle with, both physiologically and psychologically. It's a great opportunity to discover other potential issues earlier. It was for me, and it can be for you as well.

A retrospective study comparing patient notes across 4 different hospitals looked at approximately 14,000 autistic individuals and almost 2.4 million people in total to assess comorbidity rates amongst the autistic population. The analysis was done on already existing hospital data and was only looking at diagnoses that had their own ICD-9 code, meaning it would miss several conditions. But of the diseases it looked at, it found that people with autism had a significantly higher likelihood of having almost all of them. This included epilepsy, schizophrenia, bowel disorders, cranial anomalies, diabetes type 1, muscular dystrophy, Down syndrome, Fragile X and sleep disorders (Wattanasin et al., 2012).

There are numerous other studies showing that autistic children have a broad range of co-occurring disorders including ADHD, intellectual disabilities, sensory integration disorder, learning disorders, language disorders, anxiety disorder, mood disorder, depression, bipolar disorder, emotional disorder, hearing loss, cerebral palsy, mutism and visual disorders amongst other things (Levy et al., 2010).

In addition, there are studies pointing to higher risks of eczema, allergies and asthma (Magalhães et al., 2009). It has also long been "known" in the autism community that many people are getting diagnosed with Ehlers-Danlos syndrome and Fibromyalgia. But these are rare diseases in the general population, and as far as I know, there are no larger studies looking at correlation at the moment. However, smaller studies have found that general hypermobility is more common in the autistic population and suggest that further studies should look into co-occurrence of Ehlers-Danlos (Eccles et al., 2014).

Author Laura James tells her story about getting diagnosed with Ehlers-Danlos, Postural Orthostatic Tachycardia Syndrome (POTS) and autism in her book "Odd Girl Out" (James, 2017). After wondering what was physically wrong with me after more than ten years of lung collapses, torn muscles, dizziness and daily dislocations, I was finally also diagnosed with both Ehlers-Danlos and POTS right after I got my autism diagnosis. These diseases are rare in the general population, and few doctors even know their names, but if you struggle with hypermobility and pain, you should definitely mention it to your doctor.

Research on co-occurring disorders is also starting to find strong links between autism and eating disorders. One review from 2013 used 8 already existing studies to look at the percentages of autism occurring within patients who had Anorexia Nervosa. It found that the rate of autism is much higher than in the general population (Huke et al., 2013).

To try to figure out if eating disorders can mimic symptoms of autism, researchers have also done a small qualitative study to try to assess if symptoms of autism were already present before the eating disorder occurred or not. The women that were interviewed for the study reported that their social issues had been consistent since childhood, indicating that the symptoms didn't come as a result of their eating disorders (Mandy &

Tchanturia, 2015).

As someone who struggled with bulimia as a teenager, I find this very interesting. There are many theories around why someone develops an eating disorder, but I think that the struggle and stress of trying to fit into a mostly neurotypical world could definitely be a cause.

If you're already diagnosed with or think you have symptoms of any diseases I've mentioned above, I hope you discuss them with your doctor so you can get help. The knowledge of these co-morbidities can be the difference between getting proper medical treatment or being ignored by doctors for years. Don't assume that doctors know what symptoms these diseases have, or that they're common within the autistic population. If you believe you should be checked for any of the above, don't give up until your doctor refers you to a specialist to get it properly checked out. Believe me, you don't want to struggle with more pain and physical symptoms than you absolutely have to.

Sports and activities

Women on the spectrum often think they're clumsy. And that's frequently true. Lack of coordination and difficulty controlling your body is often associated with autism spectrum disorder. We're the ones who trip over our feet walking down the sidewalk, and we need to concentrate to put the fork into our mouths.

Both Kanner and Asperger described the children they studied as clumsy. Autistic children can experience developmental delays, and you already know there are several separate disorders that frequently co-occur with autism.

Disorders like apraxia, ataxia and dyspraxia can influence a person's ability to both plan and carry out different movements, and they often affect autistic people.

But even though not everyone on the spectrum will have these types of disorders, many often have issues with coordination anyways, and several studies show poor coordination amongst autistic people (Fournier et al., 2010).

With this as a starting point, being active and participating in sports can seem extremely difficult. No one thinks it's motivating to do something they're bad at. And when you see that others around you improve at a faster pace no matter how much effort you put in, it's even more demotivating.

But being active is too important for your health to miss out on. Most research points to the fact that training can improve your physical health and make you live longer. But I'm just as interested in the positive psychological changes you can get from doing it.

A recent meta-study using randomised-control trials found that physical exercise had a large effect on depression (Schuch et al., 2016). I can feel that effect myself sometimes. It's an ugly spiral. When you get depressed, you don't want to train, and when you don't train, you get even more depressed. I find that in periods where I feel down, I need to push myself to exercise, even if it's just for a little while.

Sports improve several aspects of your health, but it can also have another function for autistic people. It can help us be social and meet new people with shared interests. If you struggle with finding friends, you can join a sports centre or a class to get to know others. The people you meet there will have something in common with you, and it can be easier to develop a relationship with them.

Using sports and activities as a foundation to build friendships can be even more important when you're young.

And autistic people shouldn't give up even if being active doesn't come naturally.

I was one of the clumsy kids. Every time I ate, food was scattered all around my plate. My sweater would have stains from various sauces, and my pants were always dirty from getting pushed into muddy walls, cars or anything else I could possibly bump into when I was walking outside.

Even though I was clumsy, I participated in many physical activities as a kid. But it wasn't always a success. When I was five, I spent one week trying gymnastics, before I decided that I couldn't see the point in it. My parents then signed me up for athletics, but I was a terrible runner, and the only thing I had any talent for, was throwing heavy objects.

When my mother wanted me to take ballet classes one summer, it was as unsuccessful as the gymnastics sessions. And when we played ballgames in gym class, I was horrible. It felt humiliating to be bad at all those things. And I was an extremely sore loser, so I thought my best option was to avoid as much of it as possible. But luckily, I didn't end up hating all sports.

If you read Liane Holliday Willey's autobiography "Pretending to be Normal," you'll see her description of how she found joy in the weightless feeling of being completely immersed in water (Willey, 2014). When I first read that passage of her book, I felt such a sense of belonging because my first experiences in water were similar.

I remember writing a diary entry after coming back from the pool when I was five; I now knew how it felt to fly. The weightless sensation I got from holding my breath and floating below the surface beat anything I could experience on the ground. Feeling the weight of the water was like that long and tight hug I so sorely needed. And the peace and quiet I found underwater was unlike anything I had experienced before.

When we were dealt flyers for swimming classes in first

grade, I immediately brought it back to my dad and asked if I could sign up. And armed with a huge and bubbly yellow swim cap, I fought my way through 3 separate courses before I passed the 200-meter test and was allowed to join the swim club. I felt like a champion that day as my mum drove me home from the pool. I had swum 200 meters without a break, and it was my greatest accomplishment yet. Little did I know that during the twelve following years, I would compete and win medals in several national championships, swim a half marathon and represent my country in the Youth Olympics.

When I first joined the swim club, I was pretty bad. I regularly finished behind everyone else, and my technique was way too uncoordinated to get much progress. I would probably never have come very far had I not broken my arm when I was eleven. I spent an entire summer with the arm in a cast. And when the cast was taken off, my arm was extremely skinny and lacked muscle mass.

My dad, who was my physiotherapist when I grew up, put me on a pretty strict program to regain normal strength. At first, I was throwing medicine balls, but after a while, I was also lifting weights at a local bodybuilding studio. And suddenly it all seemed to fall into place. With the additional strength and body control, my technique improved drastically. I went from placing last to first, qualified for the junior national team and won medals at both national and international competitions.

But my performance was extremely uneven. Swimming has four main strokes you can compete in, and in addition, there's a medley which consists of all four in combination. There was an annual national competition in Norway where 18 of the best swimmers in each age group met to compete in 5 different distances and strokes to decide who was the overall best. The first year I attended, I won the competition in Butterfly, Freestyle and Backstroke, and I placed second in the Individual Medley.

In Breaststroke, however, I placed second to last, and only because one person was disqualified. My total score gave me the overall victory, but I would never become a well-rounded swimmer.

I think there were several reasons why swimming felt so right for me. First of all, it felt good to have the pressure from the water around me. As I mentioned in the chapter about sensory issues, being held tightly can feel good for someone on the spectrum. Second, the social aspect of swimming was a bit different from that of other sports. You're more alone when you train in the water. And although you swim with your teammates, there's less room for doing other things in between. Swimming felt more like a sanctuary for me where I could escape from everyone else and their demands.

Tony Attwood reports through his research on autism that sports can perfectly well be a part of someone's special interests. He believes that a person on the spectrum can perform well when they find something they truly enjoy. He mentions solitary sports such as swimming, golf, snooker, rock climbing and running as areas where he has seen autistic kids do great. And he thinks that our "single-mindedness" can lead us to success in those areas (Attwood, 2006).

As an adult, I'm extremely grateful for what swimming gave me. I got the physical foundation to lead a healthy life. It gave me the chance to master something, and it forced me to learn how to prioritise and work hard. It also got me a platform for being social outside of school for shorter amounts of time. It could still be hard going away for camps and competitions, but I did meet some people there who were more similar to me, and I think it would have been tough growing up without it.

As an adult, I tried several types of sports to take over for swimming. I lifted weights most of my swimming career, and I still do. I've tried aerobics and crashed into every single person around me (never doing that again). But I've also learned to love yoga with all its repetitive patterns (the key is a lot of youtube videos at home until you recognise which exercises usually come after each other). And I've even learned to enjoy a ball sport as I usually play tennis during the summer.

Participating in physical activities and finding something that you love doing can give you many advantages both for now and when you're older. If you haven't found anything you like yet, I'm sure you will in the future.

Food and vitamins

I've already touched upon several issues related to eating and digestion. Both bowel disorders, eating disorders and sensory sensitivities to food can make it difficult for us to obtain the nutrition we need.

In a US study, 960 children with autism were assessed for gastrointestinal symptoms and compared to a group of neurotypical peers. It turned out the children with autism were more frequently affected by diarrhoea, constipation, abdominal pain and other digestive issues (Chaidez et al., 2014). The same was found in a meta-study from the same year searching through results from 1980 to 2012 (McElhanon et al., 2014).

Several of the digestive symptoms above are now frequently labelled Irritable Bowel Syndrome (IBS) and has no single known cause. I've been diagnosed with it myself after several painful hospital visits, and I follow a low FODMAP diet which has helped my symptoms enormously. However, this means that there are several types of food I must avoid on top of the ones I struggle with because of their taste or texture.

I know I'm not alone in being concerned with having a limited diet, and if you do too, it's important you make sure you get the nutrition you need. Speak with a nutritionist or doctor if necessary. You don't want to deal with the effects of poor nutrition on top of everything else you're struggling with.

In addition to physical symptoms from lack of nutrition, certain types of food can also help you feel better mentally. A meta-study which included 10 double-blind, placebo-controlled trials found that intake of omega-3 had a significantly positive effect on depressive symptoms in people with mood disorders (Lin and Su, 2007).

Take your nutritional needs seriously, as ignoring them can hurt you long-term.

Drugs and medication

Autism isn't something that's treated with medication. And it's also not something that can be cured since it's a core part of who we are. But many of the co-morbidities that come along with autism can be medicated.

There are drugs used to help with depression, anxiety and focus that your doctor can prescribe. If you feel that taking medication is right for you, you should discuss it with a health professional and make sure that he or she looks into any side effects or possible negative outcomes from mixing several medications. When you're being prescribed medication for other conditions, it's important your doctor knows that you're autistic, as there have been noted incidents where people with autism react differently to some types of medication.

There are also drugs that aren't yet legally available to treat things like depression and trauma but are being tested for safety as well as efficiency in several parts of the world. Some popular drugs that are going through testing at the moment are for example MDMA for trauma treatment and Ketamine or

Psilocybin against depression.

Medicine is constantly evolving, so if you've tried something in the past that didn't work for you, it might be possible for you to find something else that's better able to help now.

As a teenager, I spent a year taking anti-depressants along with a cocktail of other medications my doctor thought could help me. I was very uncomfortable with it. The medications made me so tired I wasn't able to stay awake in classes at school. And I felt like I turned into a hollow and dark version of myself that didn't have the ability to enjoy even simple things like a warm summer afternoon.

After one year of suffering, I decided to quit right before I was moving away to go to college. That wasn't a great idea, and I struggled with a lot of side effects from quitting them all at the same time.

Today, I probably wouldn't have said yes to taking all of those pills without doing my own research about what they were. Although my experience with taking psychiatric medications was negative, that doesn't mean it will be for you. But you should take precautions and make sure you know what you're being prescribed. Doctors make mistakes, and they also won't know what is or isn't working for you unless you give them very detailed feedback.

Take responsibility for what you put into your body. And don't be afraid to be the person who asks annoying questions until you're entirely sure you know what you want to do.

Why you should meditate

Meditation seems to be on everyone's lips these days to treat all kinds of issues. But even though it's fashionable now, it has been around for hundreds of years. When something survives that long, it's interesting to take a look at why. Since women on the spectrum tend to struggle more with depression and anxiety than the average person, it's especially interesting to see if meditation can improve any of those issues. So what can it do for you, and what's just hype?

A US study done on a small sample of adults suffering from depression and anxiety found that after an 8-week course of mindfulness meditation, their symptoms had decreased more than what's statistically significant (Ramel et al., 2004).

A very fascinating thing to note was that the more each individual practised mediation during that period, the more they improved their symptoms. It's also interesting that most of the people in the group spent much less time meditating than they were recommended, meaning they could potentially have achieved even better results if they followed the instructions.

Some of the participants were matched with a waitlisted group, and the people practising mindfulness meditation improved their scores while the waitlisted group didn't. Unfortunately, comparing participants to waitlisted groups won't adequately show if the effect is pure placebo or not.

Like with all smaller samples, one can't draw too many conclusions from this. But the positive effect meditation has on mood disorders and anxiety in general are well documented. In a meta-study from 2010, mindfulness meditation significantly improved symptoms of both anxiety and depression (Hofmann et al., 2010).

Another meta-study from 2014 included only studies that were randomised and had a placebo group. This research also showed improvements in symptoms for anxiety and depression as well as for physical pain. However, they weren't able to show that meditation alone was more efficient than for example exercise, medication or other behavioural therapies (Goyal et al., 2014).

A similar study to the first one I mentioned in this chapter was also done with a group of 42 autistic participants. They were randomly selected to a waitlisted group or given a 9-week training program in mindfulness meditation. The participants all had symptoms of anxiety, depression and rumination. And the meditation had a positive effect on all three, as well as what is called "positive affect" (Spek et al., 2012).

So although the study isn't large enough to draw any conclusions at the moment, together with the larger meta-studies done on mood disorders for neurotypicals, this suggests that women on the spectrum can experience significant improvements in mental health from meditation.

A very small study done on three autistic teenage boys also showed that training in mindfulness reduced aggressive behaviour long-term (Singh et al., 2011). So it might be worth considering if meditation can also help reduce some of our anger issues or meltdowns. I know that I certainly have seen an improvement in both after I learnt how to meditate.

Exactly why meditation seems to be helpful isn't known, but it does have the power to change brainwaves and even the composition of the brain, which can be measured in a controlled setting. A study of long-term effects of meditation showed that experienced meditators had more grey matter in several parts of their brains compared to non-meditating peers (Luders et al., 2009).

Since this study only looked at people who had been meditating for a long time and weren't randomly picked and asked to start meditating, it can't say anything certain about the causal effect, but it can tell us that it's worth to take a closer look. And several researchers have done exactly that by setting up studies that measure differences before and after someone starts to meditate.

One study explored short-term changes in the brains of

people who started to meditate in a randomised setting. 22 undergraduates were assigned to guided meditational training for a total of 11 hours over 1 month, while 23 were placed in a control group where they were only relaxing. The researchers were able to measure a change of white matter in parts of the brains of the people using meditation, indicating that meditation could help improve self-regulation (Tang et al., 2010).

My experience with meditation has been very positive, but I think it can be hard to learn if you don't know where to begin. I had tried to learn meditation through apps on my phone for a while, but I felt like I didn't understand the goal of the practice. And I frequently fell asleep or felt very little difference no matter how often I tried doing it.

After a year of meditating daily without getting good results from it, I decided it was time to start doing some proper research into how meditation works to see if anything could improve my practice.

The first thing I realised was that meditation isn't just one technique. There are several types of meditation, and one type might be more suited to you than others. Currently, the most mainstream way of meditating is using mindfulness. Here, the meditator is supposed to focus on their breath or something else inside of themselves and empty their minds. This is the type of guided meditation you'll find in most popular apps on your phone.

Then there's a form of meditation popularly called loving-kindness meditation. Here, the meditator is supposed to concentrate on those who love them and send love and kindness to other people. It's supposed to help increase compassion and empathy and strengthen your relationships with others.

There's also a third form of meditation where you use mantras to enter a state of transcendence. By focusing on the mantra, your body relaxes and your thoughts disappear. The mantra can be said out loud or listened to, but most frequently, you repeat it silently inside your head. The mantra doesn't have any specific meaning and is often taken from Sanskrit. What it does is being your object of focus instead of your breath or your thoughts.

Some people, myself included, feel like it's easier to relax completely when using a mantra. So if you're eager to reap some of the benefits from meditation, but haven't been able to do it successfully yet, you should look into different types of meditation and see which one feels more natural to you.

There's no question that some of us with autism could benefit from more calmness, less anxiety and depression in our lives, and learning meditation could be a part of that. I try to meditate twice a day, and when I'm able to do that, it feels like time slows down the rest of the day. A warm sensation sometimes rolls over my body while I'm talking to someone, and it feels like it gives me extra time to think and process what's happening around me. Of course, I can't claim that meditation slows down time, but it makes me feel more relaxed in situations in which I'm often stressed.

My second problem with meditation in the beginning was that I kept falling asleep. And I know this is a common problem for many people who try it for the first time. They often ask what they're doing wrong. Or maybe they just think that meditation isn't for them. But you're probably doing everything right. Falling asleep means you're relaxing. However, if this happens to you every time you try to close your eyes and relax, chances are pretty high you're actually sleep-deprived and need to do something about it.

You don't sleep enough

Autistic people have a higher likelihood of struggling with sleep (Richdale and Schreck, 2009). And when we know how important sleep is to humans, we should make an effort to get enough of it.

Sleep has the highest priority amongst all my activities. For too long, my standard solution when I didn't feel like going to bed, was to just reduce the amount of sleep I had. Now, I know that if I stay up for two more hours to watch something meaningless on Netflix, I take those two hours from something I need to do before going to work the next morning. Because the eight hours required for sleep are non-negotiable.

Like so many others, I was under the impression that sleep is something boring people do. And that getting eight hours each night is only meant for children. I was so busy at work that I didn't have the time to go to bed at a reasonable hour. I started slowly by cutting my rest down to six or seven hours. And I was proud when I managed to go a week surviving on four hours as well as getting through a few all-nighters.

What I didn't know was that my mental capacity was slowly decreasing and that my performance was nowhere near where it should have been. I started getting sick more often, and when I got mono, I was completely knocked out.

It wasn't until a friend of my husband told me he had completely changed his sleeping routines after reading one book, that I started looking into sleep as a serious issue. The book he told me about is called "Why We Sleep" and is written by sleep scientist Matthew Walker. I didn't get far into the book before I was hooked – and scared.

He explained the research he has been doing both on the long- and short-term effects of lack of sleep. Just one hour missed one night will severely impair your immune system. Less sleep will affect your memory, your physical health and your ability to function properly. And it's a myth that you can get by on less than eight hours. Most people who think they can, have been sleep-deprived for so long they can't remember what it's like to perform with full mental capacity (Walker, 2017).

I'm not going to go into every single study Walker mentions in the book, but I'll recommend that you read it. It gave me such a hard reality-check that both I and my husband have completely changed our sleeping habits after reading it, and we recommend it to all of our friends.

Not only is it easy to read, but the author properly goes through experiments and methods so you understand that what he's talking about isn't only correlations, but causal relationships between too little sleep and negative health effects.

If you don't want to read the book, you should take with you that you need eight hours each night and that you can't catch up on lost sleep. You should also go to bed roughly the same time every day and get up the same time in the morning (Walker, 2017). If you're not already doing these things, now is the time to start and watch your life improve.

Autistic burnout

If you don't care to look after your health, there's a higher likelihood that you will suffer from burnout at some point in your life. But what's so special about autistic burnout? In terms of what happens when it hits you, it can be thought of the same way that athletes get overtrained or an executive hits the wall at work. But for an autistic person, it will cover all areas of our lives. It will stop us from going to work, being social, doing housework or even cooking dinner. It can completely paralyse us and stop us from participating in daily activities.

And it doesn't happen just because we worked too hard or trained too much; it happens because all the daily triggers in our lives eventually become too much. Every time we step outside we're met with a myriad of sounds, lights and smells that overwhelm us, and it takes a lot of energy trying to get through a day battling the input from all our senses.

Then there's the conscious effort of trying to fit in and understanding what's going on in every conversation we have. Not to offend anyone, to understand that someone is asking for something indirectly, or trying to understand all the subtle messages coming from a person's tone of voice. There's no wonder we try to keep everything else in our lives constant by clinging to our standard routines.

In addition to all of these things, we're still met with the same demands as everyone else in our work and personal lives. Maybe we're ok to go into battle every day for a few months or years if we're lucky. But at some point, all of these stressors will catch up with us, and our ability to cope disappears.

We'll struggle to execute tasks that we used to be able to do before with no or little help. It can seem as we become more debilitated by our autistic traits than we used to. And issues with sensory sensitivity can become much more troublesome.

One key factor here is how much pressure we or society put on us to act like a neurotypical and live up to their standards. The more we work to put on a mask, the more likely we are to be beaten down by all these stressors.

Autistic burnout can have severe consequences and can lead to us losing our jobs, spouses, friends or our homes. It can severely affect our physical and mental health as we can end up in a state where we're no longer able to take care of ourselves. I also believe that this is one of the things contributing to the high rate of suicides amongst autistic people. With a wide range between 1 and 50%, suicide attempts seem to be much more common than for the neurotypical population (Richa et al., 2014; Hedley & Uljarević, 2018; Cassidy et al., 2014; Segers & Rawana,

2014; Zahid & Upthegrove, 2017).

But unfortunately, there's no research looking into autistic burnout at the moment. In fact, when looking up autism and burnout in Google Scholar, the first hit is a study from 2003 looking at burnout amongst teachers of autistic children based on their teaching philosophy and commitment. The second is a study where they looked at the correlation between a tutor's negative biases against autistic children and burnout for the teachers, and the third is a study showing that 23 neurotypical children in 4th grade experienced signs of burnout when 2 autistic children were let into the classroom. When scrolling down, I can see no studies aimed at burnout in autistic people at all.

It is rather telling that all the studies that have been done on burnout related to autism focus on what a burden we are to the people around us rather than what our surroundings are doing to us. I think it says something about the research community's priorities and world view. Autistic people are not taken seriously as individuals, and research is not conducted on our behalf to see how we can improve our lives. It's all seen through the eyes of those that observe us and never have to live a moment in our bodies. Never experiencing the humiliation of being outside and the toll it takes on our physical health to keep up with their neurotypical demands.

We need to be kind to ourselves and our bodies when we experience symptoms of burnout. Our minds must also be allowed to rest without us feeling guilty for not participating as much as we think we should. It's better to miss out on smaller things as we go along than to let an entire life disappear because we cannot cope anymore.

But the main key to bettering our health is not to put more responsibility on ourselves to improve our situation, it also lies in society's acceptance of us as whole human beings. Maybe it starts with our families and friends, but hopefully, it spreads to acquaintances, the person we speak to on the phone or meet in the supermarket. And at some point, it must also spread to the medical and research communities. They will have to do better and look at the world from our point of view.

Self-work

For this part of the book, your task is to identify the areas where you can improve to get positive results for your physical and mental health. Write a list of the things you know you need to work on and put specific tasks into your calendar to make yourself stick to your new goals.

Ask yourself these health-related questions:
1. Do you have medical issues that you haven't gotten reviewed by a doctor?
2. How many times each week are you active?
3. Is there a sport you could try that you think you would like?
4. What does your diet look like?
5. Do you get all the nutrients you need or should you go and get checked for deficiencies?
6. Do you have gastrointestinal issues that you haven't addressed?
7. Are there medications you're taking that are making you unhappy, or that you don't properly know the effects of?
8. Do you think you could benefit from some quiet time each day to meditate? If you do, decide what time each day should be your meditation time.
9. How many hours are you sleeping each night?
10. What do you do right before you go to bed, and are they

worth risking your health for?
11. Do you fall asleep during the day or in the afternoon?
12. Which things do you need to rearrange to get enough time to sleep?

School

Why we can succeed and fail at the same time

School can be a challenge for any child or teenager. If you throw social difficulties and sensory issues into the mix, you can end up with a quite uncomfortable combination. For many, school is the first time in their lives when they're forced to spend time with people they don't like in an environment they don't enjoy.

This is why many children on the spectrum struggle with their education. But as I've mentioned before, many of us are extremely gifted. And when we're put in an environment where we can learn all day, we should initially thrive.

When I tell the story of my education, it might sound like a classic success story. In first grade, I finished my math book the first week of school and was told by the teachers to go and work on next year's curriculum on my own. Which I did, all the way to junior high. I got into the high school I wanted, and after specialising in Mathematics, Physics and Chemistry for three years, I graduated with the best GPA in school history and presumably one of the best in the country. For the remaining part of the summer, I spent time being interviewed in local and national newspapers, going on radio shows and participating in television debates discussing educational politics.

The initial interest from the media came because journalists usually pick one of those success-stories each year to showcase smart and accomplished youth. But in addition to working hard at school, I was active politically and used the attention to highlight my views.

So instead of telling the reporters that I had loved school and worked hard together with my classmates to accomplish what I did, I shared a different story. A story about how the Scandinavian school was systematically failing people like me.

Smart kids need attention too

Most autistic children are eager to learn. Just look at the efforts they put into their special interests. Many are also very smart, and this should be the perfect combination when starting school. But being highly intelligent and motivated in an environment that isn't set up to help those types of children, can be equally damaging as having difficulty learning and being ignored by teachers.

Many children with this profile eventually give up and lose their will to learn because they're not challenged or taken seriously. Many are also seen as difficult and trouble-makers. Eventually, that can lead them to drop out, or it could damage their ability to keep up long-term.

Like many gifted people with autism, I had highly specialised interests as a child. I also had the ability to go deep into anything I enjoyed. And I enjoyed pretty much every academic subject in school. I was great at maths, I loved reading, and I was competitive and ambitious.

This meant that I had a much steeper learning curve than some of my peers. But the teachers I met tried their best to keep everyone at the same level. In fact, dividing students into groups based on their performance was illegal in Norway when I grew up, and it probably still is.

Whenever we had Mathematics classes, I would sit and read and do my exercises from books the older students were using. I never asked any questions because the teachers usually ignored the high performers, so I didn't see the point.

This resulted in me learning a lot of theory, but missing several other things that the teachers would normally help you with. I did for example not learn how to formally write to show people my thought process, which first becomes important in high school or later when you're presented with more challenging problems. It wasn't at all evident to me that others couldn't just see the answers and write them down. My math skills suffered from poor form all the way to university because of this.

When it came to reading, I took it even more seriously. I started reading before I began school, and I soon developed a love for all things fiction. I could read US teenage drama books, classics like the Count of Monte Cristo, the Decameron, or extremely violent Nordic crime while I was still in elementary school. And if someone told me to read something else, I would simply refuse or get angry.

When I was around ten years old, we had reading projects where the entire class received a set of books to choose from.

The goal was to read as many as possible of the assigned books over a few months. But the books the school had chosen were far from my topics of interest.

Several of the books were filled with pictures, large fonts and stories about Danny the Dog and were written for someone who only had basic reading skills. This led me to complain loudly that I couldn't find anything I thought was even worth opening. If you prefer to read the types of books most adults enjoy, it's incredibly frustrating to be forced to read something that's meant for people who are reading for the first time.

The teachers weren't too happy about it, and they refused to give me any other options, which meant I just stopped reading altogether. My parents eventually wrote an angry letter telling them they had taken a kid who loved to read and killed all the joy she got from books. The school finally caved and let me do my own thing, and I was reasonably happy for the time the project lasted.

But that it should take that long and be that painful to be able to let a child go deeper into fields that interest them is a mystery to me. Even after my parents wrote the letter, I got sarcastic comments from teachers saying they couldn't make projects based on the interests of children who were different. Instead of celebrating individuality and encouraging gifted children to pursue their interests, they're often punished, ignored and belittled.

In other subjects, I would be asked to go and clean the school kitchen after I finished all my exercises. I would be yelled at for solving problems or reading ahead in the books, and I would never get help if I asked for it because the teachers thought I was doing just fine on my own. Being treated like that does something to a kid's self-esteem.

And it seems to be a trend that girls on the spectrum who are seen as "good students" and not acting out are getting less attention than they should (Bargiela, 2016).

Parents of children with autism today should be aware of the fact that not encouraging their strengths can be just as demotivating as if they were struggling with something they didn't understand. Children are naturally good at learning, but they need to be challenged at the right level to keep that ability alive.

Discuss this with your child. Ask detailed questions about what they think of the classes they're taking and what they're learning. Talk to the teachers. Make them understand. If they don't, try to look into other schools. Maybe even one with a different approach to learning that lets students make more of their own curriculum. Encourage them to find their special interests and let them go deeper into that. It could be their livelihood in a few years.

Respect our logical minds

In addition to not being challenged by the curriculum, I was also struggling to do things I didn't see the value of. I would always have trouble with subjects where I didn't see the purpose of what we were learning. I hated music classes for example. I was kicked out of the choir more than once because I said I couldn't care less about singing songs I didn't like the lyrics of. At the same time, the teacher would yell at me because I refused to partake when we were dancing, and I promptly told her I saw no reason to do so as it wasn't relevant to my education. I also failed arts and craft classes for not wanting to participate.

Keep in mind that this was mostly around age seven to ten, so what you see as emotionally immature responses from my side, were exactly that. I was a seven-year-old, but I had the logical mind of an adult. Just without the understanding of the world to back it up.

To make kids more interested in doing things the teachers have planned, most people use a very "pedagogical" approach to try to make the subjects seem fun. This I could only understand as one thing. The teachers were talking down to us and explaining things as if we were stupid. Not only did it make me not want to ever work with the subjects again; it also made me hate the teacher in question.

But there would have been several ways to approach a kid like me that no one tried. Show me a study that says children should learn subjects which include both halves of the brain to get optimal development. That spending time on music could increase my ability to perform in Mathematics or think of problems more creatively. Instead, my teacher said I needed to know how to sing so I could perform a lullaby when I became a mother myself. I couldn't have gotten a worse explanation, as I told her I wasn't planning on having children so her reason was irrelevant.

For children that are considered smart, and in addition are driven by pure logic as some of us with autism are, teaching needs to be approached in a different way.

Bring facts. Children understand a lot more than you think. Especially kids who like to take anything literally. If you present an argument with reasoning that doesn't apply to them, it won't bring you any further. Even today I tell people that if they're going to tell me to do something, they need to show me a meta-study with some proper credentials. If there's a study like that, I'll most of the time have no problem incorporating that wisdom into my life. If there isn't, and all you can say is that I "should" or that it's "good" for me, I'll have no sympathy for your point of view.

Today, I regret never having learnt to sing or draw properly. Kids and adults could find out that they love something they initially hated if they get proper help and can approach it from an angle that makes sense to them. If you're raising an autistic child today, be a part of explaining with facts. Both to your kids and to yourself. You might find things you're really good at and start loving something you would have otherwise never tried out.

Disobeying authorities

Have you thought about the fact that a teacher dislikes you or your child because they believe he or she is disrespectful? Many autistic children have issues with authorities, and it's natural that this will surface for the first time during pre-school or elementary school. Showing respect to someone based on their title can be extremely difficult for someone on the spectrum.

It can be even more difficult if that person is giving you orders with no apparent logical reason. "Because I said so" isn't a very good argument in autistic ears. And this is often the type of reasoning you're met with as a child. You should do something because your teacher or your parents think it's good for you.

Tony Attwood believes one of the reasons we have issues with authorities is because we don't understand when to back down, and that we won't accept a rule if we don't agree to the logic behind it (Attwood, 2006). This is reasoning I agree with completely, and it reflects my own experiences as a child and as an adult. I didn't understand the concept of "being a child" and being someone else's responsibility.

These issues materialised already in my first year of school. My teacher tried to get everyone's parents to sign our weekly homework plans. But I didn't see any point in including my parents in my homework. I did them all alone, and I didn't need their help. And if they weren't done, it would be my responsibility and not theirs.

So when my teacher told my parents at a parent-teacher conference that I didn't deliver the signed plan every week like I was supposed to, I told her I saw no reason to. She explained that it was to check that everyone did their homework. To which I responded that I always did my homework, so that shouldn't be an issue.

She then said that some of the other kids had trouble doing theirs, so she needed our parents to control that we did them. That for me was an even worse explanation than anything else, and I said she should make their parents sign their homework plans and not include me in whatever problems they had. My teacher had little sympathy for my rationalisation and said she expected a weekly signature from now on. Which she got. But just because I learnt how to perfectly replicate my dad's signature.

There were many of these episodes from pre-school until high school. I think one of my main issues was that I couldn't stand being treated like a child and being deprived of the right to make my own decisions. I hated it. The lack of control made me crazy.

But that wasn't the only thing I did that made my teachers think that I was rude or disrespectful. As very bright kids with autism usually do, I frequently corrected my teachers in front of the class, and often for tiny details they were missing.

But I hated being criticised myself, which is the case for many autistic kids. We don't understand why others don't like our criticism as we're simply pointing out facts, but we're very sensitive to any kind of corrections when they're directed at us.

We get angry and defensive, and we can spend days arguing our case and explaining why we weren't wrong. Sometimes what seems wrong to a neurotypical is also not wrong in our eyes. We tend to take things literally. That again can result in endless arguments with teachers.

One thing I struggled with was ambiguous wording during tests. In a history test, we were asked to "give examples of three things you associate with the American revolution." The teacher who wrote this was looking for known characters, important dates, consequences or interpretations of what happened after the revolution. But if you're reading this question literally, it doesn't ask for that. If I associate ice cream, butterflies and blue orchids with the American revolution, it's my pleasure to do so.

This is also something Liane Holliday Willey shares in her autobiography. She refused to go to bed on a mat when told by the teachers. And when her parents ultimately got to understand why, it was because the "mat" was actually a rug, so it wasn't possible for her to go to sleep on something that didn't exist (Willey, 2014).

There are of course nuances here. Some autistic people are so literal they can't understand what the other interpretation of the sentence is. That's the case for me sometimes, but I'm also often able to understand what someone means, but because that isn't the most accurate way to phrase it, I choose to ignore it. But although I'm technically right, it still has negative consequences for me. Other people don't enjoy it when you misinterpret them, and there are plenty of opportunities for doing so in school.

When we combine that with some of the other problems we have, we can often end up in trouble. We take things literally, we have meltdowns with too much sensory input, we refuse to accept criticism or to go along with other people's rules, and we also have a natural tendency to dislike authority figures.

This resulted in several altercations with teachers for me. Some more serious than others. I had meltdowns if I was told to stand and wait quietly until all the children were still. Why would I need to sit and wait for someone else to stop talking before I could leave the classroom?

I was also sent to the principal's office for writing a mean letter to a Mathematics teacher on the back of a test. Since I was working on a curriculum for students who were much older, I was supposed to have a different test than my classmates. But the teacher hadn't bothered to make one for me and told me to just take the test everyone else had instead of the test I had been expecting.

This was the same teacher who was mean to me during classes, not very good at his subject, and thought that he could never be wrong. It might have been an overreaction on my part to tell him to go to hell on the back of the test, but such is the nature of angry meltdowns.

Not only did the angry letter result in me going to the principal's office to discuss my behaviour with other teachers. It also resulted in him claiming that he didn't think I was particularly gifted or bright, and that the teachers at my elementary school made a mistake when they let me work with books on a much higher level. My punishment for this was that I had to go back several years in the curriculum and follow the rest of the class.

I had never been more demotivated in my entire life. And this was the day I actually stopped doing my homework. I went the 3 remaining years of junior high with a 5 instead of a 6 on all tests. All my answers were correct because I had taught myself the curriculum several years earlier. But the teacher who graded them said that since I left the tests before the time was up, it showed that I "lacked effort." But who wants to put any effort into work that they finished years ago?

Luckily, the final exam was graded by external teachers who weren't informed of who we were, so I still graduated with a 6. Later on, I graduated high school with 6 in all subjects, including all the most challenging Mathematics classes, and when I studied Finance, I specialised in Mathematical Finance and Statistics. So it turned out I wasn't bad with numbers, I just couldn't deal with not being taken seriously.

Isolation and loneliness

Teachers are often not the only people you end up having conflicts with when you're on the spectrum. Being around the other children can often be the hardest part of going to school and growing up. This sub-chapter has a trigger warning for loneliness and exclusion.

In most schools, at least where I grew up, recess meant everyone had to get out in the schoolyard. It didn't matter if it was minus 20 with a snowstorm or if the rain was pouring. Out we went, and we were supposed to play.

And most of the children loved playing. Pretending to create different worlds and take on new roles is a fun for many of them. But struggling to take part in those types of games is a key element to autism.

There are several ways that can go for someone on the spectrum. They can try to join in, but throw tantrums or get kicked out by the other children when they don't follow the rules. They can isolate themselves completely and not take part in any game. Or they can make a conscious effort trying to learn the way other children play.

Many girls are very good at mirroring their peers when they play, but their games can often be about other things than pretending. They can play with toys that they like to sort or control, and that's often not something other kids want to do.

My games, if I was at home, would consist of building with lego or sorting things for my Barbie dolls. The fun was to get everything ready and making all the pieces fit together. I would spend most of the time with my sister trying to divide the things each Barbie should own every time we played. Not a lot of girls from school found that interesting.

And most of the time, I didn't care for the games other children wanted to play. I remember how Teletubbies became popular when I was in elementary school, and I couldn't for the life of me understand what any of the other kids got out of it. When they wanted to play Teletubbies, I would either go and do something else, or I would end up in an argument with someone because I told them I thought this was childish and I didn't understand why anyone would spend time doing it. I got angry easily, and I had some pretty bad conflicts with other girls in the class because of this.

Given this behaviour, it was natural that I didn't have many friends in school. I didn't enjoy spending time with most of the people in my class, and they also didn't like to spend time with me. School was a very lonely place for me, and it's like that for many of us on the spectrum. In fact, teenagers with autism report that they're significantly more lonely than their neurotypical peers (Locke et al., 2010).

Our inclusion in social networks in school is also a lot poorer than for neurotypical children. A larger study including 75 different classrooms across Los Angeles found that autistic children had fewer reciprocal friendships than the neurotypical children. And the autistic kids seemed to become less and less connected with their peers the older they got (Rotheram-Fuller et al., 2010).

This was true for me as well. I had a small group of friends I went on adventures with the first few years in school, but I ended up more and more isolated as I kept making social mistakes. And most of the years, I spent my time with only one other person who was also considered socially awkward. We didn't have that many things in common, and she was frequently mean to me, but it was all I had.

The turning point for me didn't come until I turned 20 and finally made friends with a group of people I was studying with who shared some of my personality traits. And I think it would have been impossible for me to mask my autistic traits to such an extent that I would have been completely accepted by neurotypical children or teenagers.

So when neurotypicals think back on their childhood and romanticise the memories of easy friendships and carefree days, I feel the exact opposite. I wouldn't like to go back to being a child again. I was lonely and isolated, and I didn't experience the great joy of true friendships until I was much older.

For the younger readers who might be in this position right now, I urge you to seek out contact with support groups for people on the spectrum. Or try to join networks outside of school with people that share your interests. Because you will find people you make friends with, you just have to search a bit longer.

Group activities in the classroom

Not only does the social part of school affect our abilities to make friends outside the classroom. It can also affect us when learning. A lot of the time, classroom teaching consists of dialogues between teachers and students as well as group work. That can easily create conflicts between an autistic girl and her classmates.

Going through school without a diagnosis made things more difficult than they had to be. I was very high-performing when I could work on my own. But I was simultaneously miserable with anything that reminded me of a group project, and I didn't like working in a classroom environment.

A massive issue was that I said things in the classroom that other people found hurtful. I could correct them or argue with them. And there was no way I understood that this made the other kids dislike me.

Often, teachers would also ask for input from the class on how the learning speed was. If he or she should repeat something from the previous lesson, do a quick review, or if we were all fine just reading in the book on our own. Since I was incredibly annoyed if I needed to repeat anything, I would usually have a pretty vocal opinion about what we should do. And I frequently said that if anyone needed to repeat something that had already been said, they should do that somewhere else.

Not understanding how others could get hurt by something I said made me quite unpopular with the other girls in the class. And more than once did one of them end up in a rage or tears after arguing with me.

I soaked up every fact I read, and I fought my way through the Bible, the Divine Comedy, Ulysses and War and Peace. And every time we were discussing something related to what I knew, I wouldn't let go of a discussion until I had crushed every piece of resistance. In my mind, something was either right or it was wrong, and there was no other way to deliver information than being crass and direct. Winning arguments like that was hugely satisfying for my ego, and it got me good grades, but friends were mostly out of reach for me.

I've later learnt that it's wise to keep your opinion on sensitive topics to yourself if you want to make friends, and that delivery is everything in the neurotypical world. But I'm still horrible at it, and will frequently blurt out things that make others think I'm really rude or mean. Would I have acted differently if I had known when I was younger? Maybe. I know I try today even though I don't want to hide too much of my personality by trying to pass as a neurotypical.

The fact that the understanding of these social rules doesn't come automatically is an important reason for spending more time with someone who is growing up on the spectrum. They need to be told how other people interpret what they say and what others expect. Most likely, we also need some kind of explanation as to why the social rules are like that. Don't give up on us, but explain how neurotypicals work so we can make informed decisions on how we want to act.

It doesn't mean I think people on the spectrum should try to assimilate into the neurotypical society. Masking isn't healthy for you in the long run, and we shouldn't have to do it. But it can sometimes be helpful to know when you want to speak freely, and when a slight change in how you say something can help other people understand your point of view.

I think the ability to cut through the bullshit and be direct can sometimes be an enormous strength. And I think women on the spectrum have a great ability to question the status quo if things don't make sense and do something about it. If we're able to work on the way we deliver our opinions together with this, I think we have a lethal combination.

Are you being bullied, or are you the bully?

Another part of being in school is that we're frequently forced to spend time with kids that we don't like or who are downright mean to us. This sub-chapter has a trigger warning for bullying.

My school had several ways to try to force us to be friends with people we didn't want to play with. Each week, we had to pick a name from a hat, and this person was supposed to be our "secret friend." The teachers told us to be extra nice to them, and by the end of the week, everyone had to sit in a ring and guess who had been their friend. I didn't understand why we would do this, as it was evident that some of the kids really didn't like each other.

One week I got the name of a boy who had pushed me down a ditch a few weeks earlier. We were all told to sit in class and make a card to the person we picked. But I was completely unable to find something nice to write to someone I hated, so I wrote something else instead. My card said: "You're very nice as long as you stay far away from me."

When this boy found his card, he went straight to the teacher, and the entire class was sat down to have a serious talk about bullying and how it wasn't ok. Everyone was made to say who their secret friend was so they could find the culprit who wrote the card. When they came to his name, I raised my hand without hesitation and looked straight at the teacher. She said nothing and never mentioned the episode again.

Looking back at this as an adult who knows better, I would probably not have done this. I might have told the teacher that I couldn't write a card to this person or that I didn't want to participate. I can see that it could have been hurtful for the boy who received the card, at the same time as it wasn't fair to make me interact with someone who had bullied me. I'm not writing this to excuse myself from bad behaviour or trying to make people feel sorry for me, but I'm trying to explain what complex cases you can end up in as a kid on the spectrum. People can be mean to you, and you can be mean to them. Social interactions are hard.

But there are also cases that aren't complex. Some children get bullied just because they're different and an easy target. And autistic kids often fall into this category. There are several studies showing that children with autism are victims of bullying far more often than their neurotypical peers

(Cappadocia et al., 2011; Little, 2002).

Because I was considered one of the smart and nerdy kids, other kids in school would frequently try to pick on me. Some of the girls who were in the same grade but in a different class had a great time making up rumours about me. They enjoyed criticising everything from what I wore to how my nose looked, and they would stand not far away from me and talk loudly about how weird I was because I thought I was smarter than them. If they saw me in the hallway, they would yell things like "what's 164 times 12?!"

Most of these things didn't bother me too much, but there's one episode from elementary school that I've never been able to forget. This was done by a group of boys from the grade above mine. I was probably nine or ten years old at the time, and I was riding my bike home from school. As I was supposed to pass this group of boys, one of them grabbed my bike, so I couldn't escape. They all started to yell at me about how I thought I was so much better than them since I was using their math books. The boy holding my bike was the one I had a crush on for months, and I was devastated. When I was finally able to get away from them, I rode my bike home crying all the way.

Like most people being bullied, I never told anyone, and I would spend time praying that I would be less smart so I could become normal and be liked by the other kids.

I know my story isn't that heartbreaking. I wasn't physically abused, and I was able to stand up for myself most of the time. But I've seen many autistic children who couldn't do that. They spent their childhood being miserable because of the way both adults and other kids treated them.

This needs to stop, but it's not autistic people's responsibility alone to do something about it. Adults and kids alike all need to be educated so they're able to understand and respect each other. And as autistic kids, we need the support of adults so we get a fair chance to go through school unharmed.

Your first battle with sensory sensitivity

Another thing that's important to consider for an autistic child starting school, is that their sensory issues can become intensified in a classroom environment.

The sensory issues come in addition to spending so much energy trying to decode social rules that others get intuitively. Instead of acting out, autistic girls going to school might respond with extreme tiredness instead. They use all their energy trying not to make a social faux pas, and afterwards, there's nothing left. Imagine seeing a child struggle like that.

Many kids would be happy if they could spend time alone reading or doing something else they enjoy, but too often they're pressured into taking part in social situations that are difficult for their senses to handle.

It would make things so much easier if parents and teachers started to take kids seriously and understand that not everyone likes to be forced into social play. I think school would have been much more pleasant if the students were allowed to enjoy activities like reading and being quiet.

Being able to decide for yourself what you do has a value in itself, but it's especially important for someone on the spectrum. Not letting us do so can take a toll on our physical and psychological health. All the sensory input can eventually give us meltdowns, or we can start struggling with headaches.

My elementary school had very strict rules about what we were allowed to do, and there were no sensory-friendly activities available. Our classrooms were uncontrolled and noisy, but kids would not be allowed to wear headphones or anything else to protect them.

During recess, we had to go outside and play with our classmates. I often asked if I could stay inside and read instead, but was never allowed to do so. Instead, I brought my books with me to a storage room that was usually left unlocked and spent my time amongst old milk cartons.

I was so tired when I came home that I fell asleep almost every day. Being in a state of high alert all the time takes a toll on you, and I really wish someone had taken my sensory needs seriously in school.

If you or your child is still in school, try to have as many breaks as possible during your day where you can sit quietly and reload. Yes, it might mean saying no to social invitations. And yes, you might miss out on stuff you would like to participate in, but such is life. It's not worth pushing yourself to your limit every day. One day, you'll finally cross it, and when you do, the way back can be too long.

What happens with proper support

This takes me to the second part of my story. School wasn't all bad. It was also a source of learning things I enjoyed and getting a feeling of accomplishment.

When we think about it, school should be the perfect place for someone on the spectrum. We're so motivated to learn about things we're interested in. We also have the ability to hyperfocus, and our long-term memory and attention to detail are both good. In addition, some autistic people have lesser known abilities like being able to speak a foreign language without an accent (Attwood, 2006).

Unfortunately, social issues stop many autistic people from using their abilities properly in school. It did for me all the way from pre-school to high school. I'm not saying it was all the teachers' faults and that I couldn't have done anything differently myself. With a deeper understanding of social constructs, I most definitely would have changed many of the things I did.

But with the proper set-up and understanding from teachers, I think many autistic children can blossom. When I went to high school, I had some marvellous teachers who fit my learning style perfectly.

My math teacher was super clumsy and entirely in his own world. And he loved to discuss other applications of what we just discussed when I asked him during recess. My physics teacher was incredibly shy and made lame jokes throughout every class. Even I laughed because he was so genuine and caring about his students and the subject. My teacher in social studies and religion stood up for me against some of the girls in my class when they were mean to me. My chemistry teacher made everyone excited by constructing crazy experiments where he both explained every detail of how the reactions worked while at the same time performing something similar to a magic show.

And last but not least, my Norwegian literature teacher would approach every story anyone wrote with the most genuine compassion you could ever imagine. Not only was she an excellent teacher who led very open and inclusive classes, but she also cared so much about her students' well-being. She connected with us on a personal level and took everyone seriously.

To her, I literally owe my life. She was there for me and helped me out of a very dark place I was in as a teenager. And although I've never had the courage to tell her, she means a lot to me still. So do several of these teachers. I still think of them. Being grateful for how much they put up with and how they were able to connect with people over their favourite subjects.

School is everything when you're there. You have to stay there and you have little to no impact on how your days are set up. At the end of your education, you can either be equipped to take on the world, or you can have massive scars for life. Sometimes both. Most times both.

If you're already done with your education, the most important thing you can do is to understand how it affected you and accept that difficult situations you got into when you were young weren't necessarily your fault. You were a kid. A kid with special needs. Hopefully, you now know that you belong on the spectrum, and you can use that.

If you're currently in some form of school, there are things you can do right now to improve your learning experience. With an autism diagnosis, you will usually have the right to additional support and accommodations, which is why some people seek a diagnosis for their children in the first place. This is also often the case for older high school students or students at college and university.

Maybe you need help with deadlines, planning or bringing the right books home with you. Maybe you need a task to be explained to you in a different way. Perhaps you need help to find your way around a huge and overwhelming campus. You might also need a private space you can retreat to when you get overwhelmed. Or you just need additional support making friends and with working together in groups. Maybe you even need to work alone when it's supposed to be a group project.

You must be your own advocate to get any of these things. Ask for what you need. Otherwise, you'll have nothing. And if you ask, you might have everything. This will provide you with a base to build something for yourself and your future. University can be a dream come true where you get to dig deep into that one thing you enjoy. And that one thing could provide you with a living for many years to come.

With your motivation and ability to deeply take in a subject, you have the opportunity to become an expert in your field. It doesn't have to be theoretical. It doesn't even have to be a typical university or college subject. It can be knitting, fashion design or writing. But your education, wherever you get it, can provide you with the tools you need to truly succeed later. We just need some help to get there. And getting that help isn't bad. It's your catalyst to greatness.

Self-work

This part of the self-work can be less interesting if your education ended decades ago and you're all set in your ways. But I think it can still be helpful to identify any topics you missed out on during school.

Reframe your education:

1. Are there any subjects you hated in school because of the way they were taught that you want to look at with new eyes now? I spent last year learning how to draw, and it amazed me how something I hated so intensely during school actually was fun and educational when I tried it out again.
2. Can you in any way use the special interests you have identified to help you make learning new things more interesting?
3. Are there any special interests you could study to potentially work within your chosen field, or could you perhaps teach others?
4. Think through your experiences during school and list all the things you were good at. It might not have been things you got good grades in, but something you

intuitively understood.
5. If you're currently in a study situation, try to identify the areas where sensory sensitivity is a problem for you and make adjustments to your days or ask for help from staff at your school, as they're obligated to make reasonable accommodations in most countries.

Work

How work is different from school

Some people consider work to be an extension of school, meaning anyone with autism should have the same issues at work as they had as a student. I find that to be a gross oversimplification of the truth. A classical position as an employee in a company entails so much more both in terms of social interaction and strict control of day-to-day activities.

Going to work every day, if it's from nine to five or from seven to midnight, can be difficult for an autistic person. Many employers will require you to do all your work from a specific spot in an office. And having a fixed schedule where you have to be somewhere regardless of how you feel can be very hard. This means you'll often have more issues with sensory sensitivity than you had in university where you could usually retreat to a quiet library or read at home.

In addition to that, performance is only a small piece of how you're measured at work. When you hand in an exam to be corrected, no one cares if you're a bit awkward. While struggling to fit in socially at an office can cost you a big promotion. Going to work is a whole new set of rules you have to play by, and the consequences of breaching them or not fitting in are much more severe.

Surviving open-plan offices

The first battle many of us meet when we start working is dealing with sensory issues in an open office space. The open office design has become more and more popular in the last decade, and it has to be one of the greatest enemies of people on the spectrum. There's no noise protection and no privacy. Sometimes the offices even come with free seating each morning so you never know where you'll sit each day, making them a nightmare for someone who likes to stick to a routine.

As you have probably experienced yourself, being in the middle of a noisy room with fluorescent lights can be incredibly difficult. In addition to that, you can add the pressure of being social with your colleagues, work well with clients, and in general live up to a lot of extroverted expectations.

A great book on this subject is "Quiet" by Susan Cain (2012). She discusses the demands imposed on introverts, judging them as if they were extroverts. She discusses sensory issues and uses a great deal of science to show that for most people, those kinds of workplaces are inefficient and a massive drain of energy.

It's not a book about autistic people, but I think we can learn a lot from her writing. The issue of introverts vs. extroverts deals with many of the problems autistic people meet on a daily basis. Of course, being on the spectrum is much more than just being introverted. In fact, someone can be on the spectrum and be extroverted, although it's a rarer combination.

The long-term solution for this is actually for society to realise that most people aren't efficient in those environments. And that for many of us, it can be harmful to our health. Before that happens, I suggest you invest in a good pair of headphones if you work in any kind of office job where you need to concentrate in front of a computer.

Trapped by execution

We've already discussed executive functioning in chapter 7. And the same way it can have a large impact on someone's personal life, it can also cause trouble in your career.

For many people, executive functioning is a core part of their job description. Planning and coordinating things for customers, replying to emails in a timely manner and finishing all your projects on time.

My one greatest tip for overcoming issues with executive functioning at work is to keep a meticulous calendar. Whenever something pops up, you don't have to deal with it right away, but you have to decide when you'll do it. This should go into your calendar. First of all, so you don't forget it. And second of all, so you have set aside time to finish the task.

I include absolutely everything in my calendar. Not only things that need to be read or done, but if I know I need to check that someone else has done their job, it goes in my calendar as well. Are you expecting a delivery? Put it in your calendar so you know to follow up if it hasn't arrived by that time.

You can include all kinds of details you need to remember about a task. And if it's a large project, you can make it a recurring event where you update several workstreams. When the notification pops up on your screen, you'll know exactly what to do. And if you don't have time to do it at that time, you can reschedule it for later.

In chapter 7, I shared several of my struggles with executive functioning in my personal life. But for some reason, I don't have all of the same issues with this when I work. And today I've made it a large part of my career to lead a deal team through long and complicated processes.

This didn't come automatically though. When I started out as an investment banker, I had to learn the hard way. As you climb your way up the banking hierarchy, leading projects and being in control is most of your job. And after making a fool of myself more than once because I had missed something, I started making rules and building systems to be able to catch anything. And it worked. When I'm at work, I reply promptly to any calls or emails that come my way, and I get things done.

The things I miss out on are usually things I have trouble figuring out. For example filling out predefined forms. The alternatives rarely cater for all possible answers, and I'll frequently give up halfway because it's too hard. It took me a year to fill out the entire form I needed for health insurance the last time I changed jobs. There were just too many ambiguous questions where I didn't know what to reply.

But execution at work isn't something only autistic people struggle with, and in some ways, we can use our abilities to perform better than the average person. As you remember, we're on often better at spotting small details, which can be a huge advantage in several jobs. Catching an incorrectly formatted powerpoint slide is surprisingly difficult.

Autistic people also have a greater ability than neurotypicals to process things when the information load is high. This means that your ability to hyperfocus might not only work for your special interests, but also for more mundane tasks (Remington et al., 2012).

If there are specific things you struggle with, you can also ask your boss for accommodations. Maybe it helps you to see a task in writing instead of being told what to do over the phone. At the end of this chapter, you'll find suggestions for this and other accommodations you can ask for in the office.

When you're not a team player

Being well-liked and mastering social situations can become even more important at work than it was in school. Company politics are often affected by who is seen as more likeable. Who can play the game, and who can make sure no one gets their egos hurt or toes stepped on. And the games people play are often steered by social nuances instead of trying to do what's right.

This can be difficult to swallow. For us, things are black. Or they are white. There is nothing in between, and certainly no other colours. By sticking to your principles at work, you can come across as not willing to compromise or accommodate other people's point of view.

This combined with being very direct and not often showing happiness externally can make an employer think of you as a bad fit. I already mentioned that I was called a bitch by my first boss, but he meant it as a compliment and said it was the only way for women to survive in finance.

But he's not the only boss who has complained that my natural way of being is off-putting to others. One of my other bosses said it was general knowledge within the firm that I was cold, too direct and not liked by anyone. He also said I came across as arrogant because I would promptly point out a mistake in front of other people.

I wasn't able to play the game as well as the others, and I didn't understand what I was doing wrong. I didn't want to be mean, but I couldn't pinpoint exactly what I was doing to piss people off.

To get to the bottom of this, I spent some time studying the people I worked with. Their language was fundamentally different from mine. It contained a lot more automatic pleasantries and smiles than I was comfortable with. And people kept asking each other questions when they didn't care about the answer. They also made suggestions instead of saying that something was wrong.

Slowly, I tried incorporating some of their routines into my own habits. I tried smiling every time my eyes linked with someone, and sharing fun stories in the kitchen. I offered to help my boss when I saw that he was busy, even if I knew what he was doing didn't need my input, and I learnt not to say that I disagreed, but rather suggest what could improve if we did it differently.

It made people I work with like me better, but the more I tried, the more it felt like I was wearing someone else's face, and that the words I was saying were coming from some pre-made tape recorder. As I've done earlier in my life, I was putting on a mask because neurotypicals were uncomfortable with the real me.

I ended up getting more and more frequent headaches and had to call in sick several times a month because of it. I realised that faking my way through the social niceties at work isn't sustainable. So now I've tried to dial it back to a level I think I can live with.

I'm not certain that I can hold it up forever, but as long as I'm not my own boss, I have to do it to some extent. This is what many autistic people do to fit into a neurotypical world. And even if we make it work, it can consume our lives and health in return. To be able to work without doing all of these things, you need to choose the right career and the right firm.

Choosing the right career

Finding the right job means finding something that interests you. But it's also important that you choose a job where you won't struggle with too difficult demands in terms of socialising or executive functioning that you can't meet. This can mean looking at a different career path or just finding a company that caters for your needs.

Finding a job that lets you use your strengths is important for everyone, but perhaps even more so for autistic people. By definition, we have an uneven profile of strengths and weaknesses, so we want to make sure we choose something we're good at. If the job we find at the same time can let us be the right amount of social and cater to our sensory needs, we're golden.

Choosing a field of work that coincides with your special interests can be a great way of using your strengths where they're needed the most. It can be the difference between a highly fulfilling life and one in which you're unhappy every day.

There seem to be some typical roles that are more common for autistic people to be successful in. For example jobs where you need to work alone and can spend time deeply focussing on one thing at a time. Artistic roles like acting or writing also seem to be very popular.

If you're more sensitive than the average, you can have a special gift or way of seeing things that sets you apart from everyone else. Many can have successful careers within research roles supported by the fact that we're so attentive to details, and that many of us love to go deep into subjects we care about.

Getting accommodations at work

In most countries, your employer will be legally required to make reasonable accommodations for you if you're autistic. This can sometimes be tricky if you don't have an official diagnosis, and for some, the prospect of getting work accommodations can be the reason they pursue one.

But to get those accommodations, you also need to be open about being autistic. Many people who have a diagnosis aren't comfortable sharing that at work, even if it's just with their boss or an HR department. Some of them are afraid of being judged, while others think they won't be taken seriously or that they will be discriminated against later.

I don't think there are any right or wrong answers here. If you don't want to share that you're autistic because you're afraid of being treated differently, that's perfectly fine. You're not obligated to tell anyone. There's also no obligation on your part to inform anyone during a job interview or before you start in a job.

If you decide that you're not comfortable sharing your diagnosis, there are still things you can ask for to make your life easier at work. You can discuss some special accommodations for noise without backing up your needs with an autism diagnosis. It's perfectly ok just to say you're particularly sensitive to certain sounds and that you need some way of avoiding too much of it to work efficiently.

If you're comfortable letting HR or your boss know that you're on the spectrum, there are other specific things it can be helpful to talk about. You can discuss your specific strengths and weaknesses to get projects or task that are tailored to what you can do well. And you can make even more adaptions to your work environment to meet your sensory needs.

Other accommodations you can consider to ask for is to get clear, written instructions, do some work from a home office or spend less time in staff meetings. It all depends on what your issues are and what your workdays look like. The person who diagnosed you can also make written recommendations of what to adjust, and you can bring this with you.

If your company refuses to make accommodations, there are several organisations you can contact for help depending on which country you live it. Because the fact is, that even though firms are legally required to make reasonable accommodations for you, some firms will still refuse to do so.

Self-work

Use the self-work section of this chapter to think through if there are other potential career paths you would like to explore, or if you need any accommodations in your current job.

Improve your work-life:

1. Are there any of your special interests you could turn into a career?
2. In what areas are you highly skilled?
3. Are you a good leader and organiser, or do you prefer working for someone else who does those things for you?
4. Do you want to have a lot of social contact at work, or do you have a strong preference for working alone?
5. If you're already employed somewhere, would it help if you shared your diagnosis?
6. Is your workday optimal to help you perform at your

best, or do you need any types of accommodations?
7. Do you struggle with sensory sensitivity at your place of work? And if you do, what could be done to improve them?
8. Are there any executive functioning tasks you need assistance with?
9. If you're unhappy, are there other jobs you could look for where you think this will be different?
10. Are there any groups that help autistic people with work accommodations or training in your area?

Sex and relationships

Who we are attracted to

Do autistic people fall in love? That's a question I've seen too many times, as many people assume we're incapable of connecting with others. The short answer is yes. We do fall in love and we're perfectly capable of having intense feelings for someone. But some of us are also asexual or aromantic. We have the same differences within our group as neurotypicals. But we have a tendency to be more varied, and there are fewer autistic people who identify as straight.

An online study from 2017 showed that women on the spectrum had a higher likelihood of being either asexual, bisexual, lesbian or have other types of attractions that were different from heterosexual. The study separated attraction, sexual contact and sexual identity. And while there was a statistically significant difference on the reported numbers for attraction, the difference wasn't significant for sexual contact or sexual identity. This can mean that not everyone acts on their attractions (George and Stokes, 2017).

I have no trouble believing that other types of sexuality are more common within the autistic community. And that reflects the way I identify myself as well. I've been in relationships with both men and women, and I feel like I'm more attracted to someone's personality than the way they look.

How a person looks doesn't seem to bother me that much, and I've dated people who have been considered both gorgeous and ugly by my friends. If I'm attracted to someone's mind, I'll automatically think that they look good. I also don't care about gender.

I've realised that there are several little things about a person that can attract me to them. An impressive intellect, their ability to argue complicated issues or an interest in a field we both enjoy. Since our special interests are such a big part of our lives, I don't think it's unnatural that we often fall for someone who can share our joy or who can deepen our knowledge in other areas.

How someone affects my senses has also had a big impact on my dating preferences, and smell seems to be the most important factor. I've found myself falling for someone wildly inappropriate just because their scent was heavenly. I've also struggled in relationships with someone I didn't enjoy the smell of, and it ended because I didn't want to be physically close to them.

I've had long-term relationships where the sexual attraction always seemed forced. It could be the way they tasted, or how they touched me. The feeling of discomfort was there through the entire relationship, and if I would have just listened to my instincts from the beginning, I could have saved us both a lot of trouble. With our sensory sensitivity, I think it's extremely important that we notice how we react with a partner.

I stayed for six years in a relationship with someone I wasn't physically attracted to just because I didn't take my sensory needs seriously. Luckily, with my current husband, I love the way he tastes and smells. And I can lie next to him and smell his chest for hours.

When it comes to who we're attracted to, I think we just need to pay attention to what our bodies are already telling us. And no one should let anyone else dictate their relationships.

And on that note, I think it's interesting to look at what happens when two people who are on the spectrum date. I think that can lead to a wonderful dynamic where two people understand each other very well.

As mentioned in chapter 3, autistic people seem to be a lot better at communicating with each other than with neurotypicals (Crompton, 2019). And we also tend to choose other autistic people as our best friends (Locke et al., 2010). So it's not that unnatural to think that we often end up dating someone else on the spectrum.

I've dated people on the spectrum before, and it has been very nice. We've had our own issues, but understanding each other socially wasn't one of them. When dating a neurotypical, our different needs for social contact and expectations have often been a problem.

But it's also perfectly normal for someone on the spectrum to date a neurotypical person. We're all individuals with different needs, interests and feelings, and only you can decide if a person is right for you.

Managing the dating scene

Since one thing that defines autistic women is our atypical communication style, it's only natural that this extends to dating as well. This means that romantic relationships can be affected by the way our brains are wired.

In the initial phase of meeting someone you're attracted to, there's traditionally some game-playing when trying to figure out if you like each other or not. That phase can be very difficult to manage for someone on the spectrum. Hidden meanings, unwritten rules and holding back when what you really want is to be all in from the start.

One of the things neurotypicals seem to agonise over when going out for the first time is where to take the person they're dating. Do you say where you want to go or do you let the other person choose?

If you're autistic and have a strong preference for where to go because of noise sensitivity, you might not have the option of letting the other person casually decide where you go for your date. But will the other person then think you're controlling or weird if you turn down their suggestion to go to a bar with a neighbourhood quiz? That's a possibility. But you probably wouldn't be happy in a relationship with someone who couldn't accept that you want to go somewhere quiet anyways.

There also seems to be a lot of games where people hold back on showing their personality to not scare the other person away. Do you act coy to keep some of the secrecy in your relationship early on, or do you say what you mean in every case? I've found that I lose many people early in the dating process because I offend them or come across as extremely opinionated. But that's also who I am. And I think showing this as soon as possible is a better option than trying to please someone in the beginning when you're probably going to be wrong for each other long-term.

Sometimes, it can be helpful to understand dating rules, but you shouldn't take it too far to try to please the person you're seeing. You're also allowed to protect your own boundaries and let the other person know when something about your date is making you uncomfortable. If some places make you queasy or give you sensory overload, you should freely tell the other person that you don't want to meet there.

Another thing I've noted about autistic women when we date is that we tend to get overly excited if we feel that we connect with someone. Things get intense very fast, and that can scare our love interest away.

In some cases though, the affection we feel can also make us cross over to stalking or obsessing over the person we have feelings for. And I would like to stress right now that anyone who crosses that line should aim to get professional help, as the consequences can be severe for both parties if you don't. The person being stalked and bothered will obviously have an issue in their life, and it can be incredibly scary for them. The person doing it might be prosecuted for it if they don't stop, and trying to engage in a relationship with someone who doesn't want you in their life can be very painful.

Of course, I realise that there are cases in between where you send a few too many texts because you didn't read the other person's signals, but that will happen to most people at some point in time.

I've had a few embarrassing incidents myself. A few years back, I went on a fantastic tinder date. His profile was perfect. He was tall, dark, incredibly good looking, interested in politics, smart, enjoyed good wine and had a serious interest in literature. We had been texting for a while, and when we met up at a bar, we ended up spending the next 24 hours together. I felt a passion I hadn't experienced in a long time. We had two more dates like that, and I thought I had found my perfect match.

I was the one initiating both dates after the first, and I was also texting him frequently between the dates. Before our fourth date, he told me he had to reschedule. And when he finally texted me again a few weeks later, he told me that it had been way too intense for him and that he needed space. I was hurt, but also ashamed that I hadn't understood that what I felt wasn't mutual. It didn't take me long to get over it, but the shame is still lingering long after. And he's not the only one who has suddenly pulled back because I seemed too eager.

When going through those dating experiences and getting disappointed again and again, I've had two choices. Either, I try harder to contain myself to more socially acceptable standards, or I'm open about what type of intensity I need at the beginning of a relationship and realise that someone who doesn't want that isn't right for me.

I think the answer lies somewhere in between. It was probably healthy for me to learn to focus on other things in my life than dating. This gives you time to properly consider if the person you're seeing is a match for you, or if the butterflies are just camouflaged excitement from getting attention from someone new. But in general, I think it's better to be honest and upfront about what you like and lose some interested parties early on instead of doing something that doesn't come naturally to you.

Not all of our quirks are negative when we're trying to date in a neurotypical world though. I also feel that we often have an advantage, and I know there are other autistic women who feel the same. We can be so honest. We can drop the act, the games, and the drama and tell people exactly how we feel.

When I date, people either find me extremely fascinating or despise me from the start. And I've been told by many people I've dated that I'm the most refreshing breath of air they've met in a while. If someone asks me a question, I'm usually way too honest. And in dating, that sometimes seems to be an advantage because people are so tired of the games and the pretending.

But some people on the spectrum seem to be excluded from

dating and relationships altogether. It seems to be especially common that autistic men complain about not having girlfriends or partners. Some women experience the same, but on average we're more often in relationships or have a family.

One Norwegian study who followed 74 autistic children for 17 to 38 years found that 99% were unmarried as adults (Mordre et al., 2011). However, this is a study based on children who were diagnosed from the 1960s until the 1980s, and the report classified 71% of the autistic population as having IQs lower than 70, so the numbers aren't necessarily correct for the general autistic population. And I most certainly don't think it accurately reflects the diversity of relationship statuses you'll find in autistic communities.

In the UK, the Adult Psychiatric Morbidity Study from 2007 found that there were a lot more autistic people amongst the unmarried population than amongst those who were married, divorced or widowed. However, this trend was only identified for men (Bebbington et al., 2009).

If you want to date, but feel like you're not able to. This can, of course, be very difficult. But no one owes us a date no matter how we act. If we want a partner, we also have to be attractive to the other person. That can be a hard reality to accept, but we're also able to work on ourselves and reach out to get help with dating if we need it.

It can also be very helpful to define the type of person you would like to attract for dating. There are some exercises at the end of the chapter that will help you do that. The point is to be clear about what you want and then figure out how you can get that. If you're looking for someone who will spend quiet evenings at home with you, trying to go to a bar to meet them is probably not a great strategy.

Enjoying sex when your senses are sensitive

It's not only the social aspects of dating and relationships that can be different for someone on the spectrum. Sex can come with its own set of challenges too. And the first thing that might make sex difficult for an autistic person is sensory sensitivity.

For me, light touches have been an issue, and this is frequently the case for other people on the spectrum as well. Light strokes are uncomfortable, and it can feel like someone is trying to tickle us. And many of these types of touches are common when people have sex. Some specific things I dislike, that I know most other people would enjoy is for example when someone gently places their hands on my nipples or the inside of my thighs. What other people think is light foreplay feels like torture to me.

It wasn't until I started researching autism that I realised this was an issue other people had as well. I had assumed the only reason I was uncomfortable was traumatic incidents in the past. Since they happened when I was very young, it can be difficult to tell the two apart, and to some extent, it probably is a combination of the two.

If you dislike a particular type of touching, this can be confusing for a partner who is used to getting positive responses when they touch someone that way. They likely haven't experienced this with others previously, and I'm sure it can feel very disappointing when something they do to give their partner pleasure only annoys him or her.

I know this has been the case for my husband. Not only is it confusing and difficult for him not to do something he has always done, but it's also disappointing since he has to avoid things that he enjoys doing. If that happens, I think it's particularly important to be open with your partner and tell them that this is very common for someone on the spectrum.

It can be helpful to show them literature on the topic. A simple Google search will often suffice as long as they're interested in reading what they find. What isn't an option is letting your partner ignore your preferences because they're unable or unwilling to learn.

You should spend time talking through your boundaries, and explain what doesn't feel good to you. You might not even know everything you don't enjoy at the moment, so when new things come up, you must not hesitate to let your partner know. It's easy to get pushed into doing something that's uncomfortable for you because you think you should like it. But with the understanding that you're not the only one experiencing discomfort in those situations, it can be easier to manage.

We must also look at the positive things autistic people can get out of sex. You probably have some kinds of touching that feel good to you. And you shouldn't be afraid to explore that. For me, and many other women on the spectrum, this is deep pressure. Maybe you'll enjoy it if your partner gives you a massage, or in general has a firm grip?

I sleep with a weighted blanket because I like the feeling of being grounded. That sensation is exactly what you can get by having someone lie on top of you during sex, so don't despair if there are things you don't like. You probably have plenty of things you really enjoy.

Another thing that I find interesting to explore is combining different sensory inputs. During sex, I think you can experience a lot more pleasure from doing this. Play some music that you usually feel in your entire body. It will probably feel surprisingly good the first time you try it.

Developing a good sex life with someone is all about being

open and letting them know how you feel. And here we have another advantage since we're often used to being straightforward and honest. I've never had an issue with talking openly about sex and attraction. I treat it like most other topics I'm interested in. Use that to your advantage if it works for you. Many people will find it both refreshing and enticing that you can talk so freely about sex.

However, make sure you don't tell personal things about your sexual life to people whom you don't trust on a personal level. It can be used against you or be misconstrued if someone believes you're doing this to flirt or hit on them.

I have to finish the part about sex by making it clear that every person on the spectrum is different. Some of us enjoy sex and some of us don't. If you're in a relationship with an autistic woman, you need to talk to her to figure out what she likes. Just like with every other partner you've had in your life.

Building lasting relationships

When you're in a long-term relationship with someone, the small problems you had when you were dating seem to either go away or become magnified. Since you spend so much time together, your partner will see you in all sorts of states, and they can either be a support, or they can make you feel worse.

I've been married twice, and the first marriage was a clear example of how things can go wrong. We met when I was 19, got married when I was 24, and by the time I was 25, we filed for separation.

But the problems between us were with us all the way from the beginning. First of all, I didn't know myself very well at the time. I was struggling with eating disorders, PTSD, and in general low self-esteem and depression. Autism wasn't on my radar back then. The only thing I knew for sure was that I didn't fit in with other people.

I had never lived with anyone before, and I had very poor skills when it came to cleaning, cooking and washing clothes. I also refused to change any of those things and thought that he was the one with an obsessive relationship with cleanliness.

That was one obvious thing that made us a bad fit. But we didn't properly talk about any of our problems, which made them worse. When we started arguing, he got extremely angry, and I clammed up completely. Most of the times we were fighting, there was something bothering me, but I felt it was stupid to share my insecurities, and that it would make me look weak and vulnerable.

One example is from when I first moved in with him. He threw all my furniture away because it didn't fit with the style of the apartment. And all the walls were filled with pictures of his friends and family, with no room for me. I told myself that this was a very stupid thing to be upset about, and I didn't dare to tell him. Had I had the guts or the knowledge to sit down and discuss that I needed some space, we could potentially have found a solution to most of our arguments.

During the time we lived together, he was also displeased with the fact that I seemed to have no interest in decorations or helping pick new furniture for the apartment. I wasn't very good at it, but the reason I never wanted to give any input was that I couldn't afford to buy any of the things he wanted.

You see, I was very young and still in school. I financed my life with a student loan, part-time jobs as a journalist and some help from my grandparents. Most of my student loan went to paying him rent, and there wasn't much left for shopping, travelling or eating out. All things that he loved to do and could afford. He was older and working in a very well-paying job at the time. And although he liked spending money, he didn't like to share. And I never had the guts to tell him that it put me in a very difficult position.

It was very frustrating that I had to save for weeks or months to be able to pay 50% of a dinner when he wanted to go out. And sometimes, I couldn't afford to go on holiday with him, which would make him very angry.

The last summer we were together, when we had lived together for almost six years and had gotten married the year before, we had a huge argument because of this. I had to spend my last money buying two suits since I started working in the fall, and he was upset that I wouldn't rather spend that money on a trip to Paris. This was the first time during our relationship that I had the guts to talk about something that made me uncomfortable. I told him that if he wanted us to do things that I couldn't afford, he would need to cover more than his share. That summer, he did take me on a trip to Paris, and he also paid for a few dinners.

My fear of talking about sensitive subjects made things very difficult throughout our entire relationship, but it wasn't what finally broke us. We were extremely different and didn't want to spend time doing the same things.

He hated literature and reading, and he would get anxious if he had to do anything related to numbers. And while I was introverted and socially awkward, he was extroverted and good with people. He had a strong sense of fashion and style, while I was mostly wearing sweatpants. Some of those things were great. He introduced me to friends, hosted parties, and helped me go from wearing pyjama pants outside to having fashion as a special interest.

But the intellectual parts of the relationship were missing. I would have loved to discuss books, finance and ethical issues with someone I was in love with, but he never wanted to try. With increasing disdain, I was looking outside our relationship to find those things, and I realised way too late that we needed to break up. Thinking back on it now, there are so many things I would have changed if I could, and those things I try to do right in my current marriage.

I realise that we probably shouldn't have been together in the first place, and we certainly shouldn't have gotten married. A few days before our wedding day, my maid of honour asked me if I was sure I wanted to go through with it. And instead of saying yes, I asked: "who else would love me?" That's extremely sad to think back on, and I assume it's something that many women believe at some point; that they're so difficult, and so unlovable that only the person they're currently with would stand to be with them.

With my current husband, the journey was very different. I was older and knew myself better. I had gone through a long period of being single and only dating for shorter periods. From this, I had learnt what to look for in a relationship, and which things could turn it into a complete disaster.

We met at work and clicked instantly. I thought he was a bit annoying, but he was so similar to me. I told friends that I was working with the male version of myself. He isn't autistic, but we both think he's neurodiverse somehow. We think in the same way, we love reading and learning new things, and we're both honest to the core. When we started dating, we agreed that we would always tell each other what was wrong and help each other improve. We share what we feel, and we show each other compassion.

I think it's extremely important to find a partner who is willing to work on things with you. Being in a relationship can feel great. You can learn about each other's communication styles, and support each other in difficult situations. And best of all, you get to feel loved.

I can relax in peace and quiet with my husband, and being

with him doesn't drain my energy. If I'm tired, I can sleep next to him, and I enjoy the social contact we have when we're both home from work.

But even though all of these things sound great, it doesn't mean that we don't have issues we need to work on. I'll get super annoyed if he chews too loudly or touches me in a way that I don't like.

Sometimes, my husband will be the person triggering me. He'll keep touching me when I'm sensitive or think it's too much, and he will be imprecise in his communication or he can disturb my routine. And when he does those things, not only will it make me angry and potentially trigger a meltdown, but it makes me feel like he doesn't take me or my condition seriously. But the truth is that it's hard for someone else to change their behaviour to suit us. And it's not fair if our partners always have to adjust.

The important thing is that you talk about how you solve it when you want something to change. That's why my current husband and I always try to talk about what triggers our arguments. We look at what each of us was doing before it started, and we see if there are any routines we can change to make sure it doesn't happen again.

We spend time figuring out what rules we want to have in our relationship, and I think that's an easy thing everyone could do.

So how often should you sit down and have a discussion about rules? Pretty often, I think, but the most important time in someone's relationship would be when they move in together. Two people who cohabitate will need to cooperate in many areas, and if you don't talk about your expectations and set some rules, it will be difficult to live together.

But for you to be able to be happy with someone else, you also have to work on yourself. Before getting diagnosed, many of the issues you experience in a relationship can feel confusing. We have meltdowns, sensory issues, and can be rigid or come across as mean. Knowing that you have a diagnosis and understanding what drives your issues, can have a huge positive impact on your relationship.

Self-work

I think it can be helpful to separate the tasks for this chapter into dating and long-term relationships, as the issues faced in those situations can vary widely. Start by defining the type of person you would like to date so you can better recognise them in real life.

Define the partner you're looking for:
1. What interests would you like to share with a partner?
2. What do they like to spend their time on?
3. Which discussions would you like to have?
4. Are they introverted or extroverted?
5. How important are looks?
6. What personality traits do you appreciate?
7. How much time do they want to spend with you?
8. What type of relationship are you looking for?
9. Do they want kids or pets?
10. Are there any dealbreakers?

For someone you're already living with, it can be helpful to have discussions about topics that could become issues so you know what each of you expects.

Work on your relationship rules:
1. What does each of you want to spend your time on? If

you have agreed to prioritise certain things, remember that this means you sometimes also have to say no to the things you didn't put on your list.
2. Discuss how often you want to be with friends, and when it's ok to have people over. This is especially important for those who get easily tired by being social, which is most of the women on the spectrum. Let your partner be aware of when it's too much for you and when you need him or her to either bring friends elsewhere or ask them to leave.
3. Talk about your budgets. Be open about what each person earns and if you think it's fair that you cover your own expenses or if the person making more should also pay more. When that's settled, you need to discuss what you want to spend your money on. How much do you want to save, and for what are you saving? How much goes to apartment, holidays, clothes, food and hobbies?
4. Have a plan for how to deal with meltdowns both if they're in public or at home. I need to be left alone when that happens, and potentially leave the place I'm currently at. It might be different for you, and you know this best. Share it with your partner when you're not angry or upset so you can have a plan for what they can do when it happens.
5. Who is responsible for what in the household? Does one person always do dishes or the laundry or is it the person who used the things last who has to do it?
6. What does cleanliness mean for each of you? Do you have different standards that will make it difficult to please both of you at the same time? Will you be able to work on cleaning together, or will it be a source of conflict that you can remove by hiring someone?
7. What do you do if you need to move the other person's

stuff? I've told my husband and my cleaner that if they think any of my things are in their way, they should collect them and put them on the kitchen table or in a basket in the bedroom. That way, I can put them where they belong, and I won't need to have a meltdown because my things are missing.
8. Agree on what type of communication style you're both comfortable using. I prefer honesty and explanations to excuses or apologies. My current partner is the same way, and we have agreed that we'll always be honest about things each of us can improve to make life better for both. It means we both have to swallow our pride from time to time and acknowledge that we can improve, but that's also what makes it work.
9. What type of physical contact do both of you enjoy? Are there any types of touching you want to avoid, or do you have any triggers that your partner should be aware of?

Being abused

Women on the spectrum are easy targets

Women and girls on the spectrum can sometimes be described as naïve. We're also honest and open-minded, and most of us struggle with social cues and understanding other people's intentions. Those things together can make us easy targets for unknown predators, and autistic women have a high likelihood of being raped or assaulted.

Some studies show that autistic children have a higher likelihood of experiencing a broad range of bullying and abuse. But as adults, it seems like we mainly have a higher risk of being sexually assaulted (Weiss and Fardella, 2018).

In Sweden, a long-term twin study revealed that girls with symptoms of autism were three times more likely to experience sexual abuse than neurotypicals (Gotby et al., 2018).

The study was following twins throughout their lives, and

when they were nine years old, their parents were interviewed about their symptoms. When those twins turned 18, they were asked to fill out a questionnaire about sexual abuse. To make sure that the symptoms of autism weren't caused by early sexual abuse, the researchers only included individuals who were sexually assaulted after they were nine years old.

The study also separately looked at twins who shared 50% or 100% of their genes with their sibling. Since the twins grew up in a similar environment, one could assume it would be possible to predict if the risk for abuse increased based on genetical factors or not. According to the results, increased risk of being sexually assaulted was mainly driven by genetical factors (Gotby et al., 2018).

The results are disturbing, but not surprising. When you struggle reading other people's signals, and in some cases have difficulty understanding their intentions, you'll be an easier target. In addition, some predators look for people who stand out from the crowd or who seem different. Autistic people can also have fewer friends to get support from, and they're not always comfortable asking for help from others.

It makes us easy victims. Since we often feel that something isn't right in social situations, we also learn to not trust those signals. We teach ourselves that to get by, we need to suppress our emotions and do things that feel uncomfortable and unnatural to us. When we're trying to navigate social rules, we rely on books, movies, or observing how others act in a similar environment. We lack the inner guidance we can trust to tell us when something isn't right.

This is why, when other people hear us describing dangerous situations, they'll wonder why we didn't pick up on the signals sooner. Why didn't we understand that he was hitting on us? Why didn't we walk away before anything happened? Maybe we were uncomfortable, but because we've been taught by society that in order to not be rude we need to follow other people's lead, we stay.

Do I think that this means all autistic women need to "get their act together" so they don't end up in those situations? Not at all. I think it's something we should try to be aware of, but most of all I think society needs to change and take women's issues seriously.

Going back to the small qualitative UK study I've cited several times in the book already, 9 of the 14 women who were interviewed reported that they had been sexually abused (Bargiela, 2016).

They seemed to have some of the same thoughts about why they had been abused. Some believed that they had difficulties understanding other people's malicious intentions, and others reported not understanding that they were flirting because they were only trying to mimic the men's behaviour to fit in.

Another reason that was mentioned was that they had difficulty asserting themselves because they so frequently did things they didn't want to in order to be accepted by society, and it was difficult to know how to say no before it was too late.

Several women reported to have learnt from the incidents, and that by understanding how to assert themselves, they would now choose to leave a situation if they noticed they were being pressured into something they didn't want. Some also said that the diagnosis of autism had helped them to get the tools to navigate these situations better and to understand when to ask for clarifications, and that it was ok for them to walk away or say no without explaining themselves to others (Bargiela, 2016).

And I think that's key to remember here. We shouldn't spend time trying to learn how to fit into a neurotypical society and lose ourselves in the process. Instead, we should explore our needs and learn how to set healthy boundaries. And we should know that we have the same right to feel comfortable in social situations as everyone else.

The remaining part of this chapter will contain descriptions of sexual abuse, rape and violence. If you're not comfortable reading about that, you should skip to the self-work part, which covers setting up new boundaries.

Predators you don't know

Like many other women on the spectrum, I've experienced abuse more than once. When I was a teenager, I didn't have many close friends. I also didn't have any adults to talk to about personal things.

Internet wasn't new at that point, but social media was, and this was long before Facebook. Because I wanted to make friends, I registered a profile on a small social media site connected to a newspaper. It had a picture, information about my age and gender, and people could message each other.

One man kept messaging me several times over a few months. I didn't reply to him at first, but he kept coming back. We started talking, and after a while, I began telling him more intimate things. I shared the fact that I was attracted to other girls, but had no experience. He told me that he used to date a girl the same age as me and that she had felt the same way.

I never saw a picture of him, as he was always "too busy" to send one, but he saw several of me, including the one I had uploaded to the site. He called himself Robert and used a last name that's very common in Norway, and I started to like him.

I shared personal things with him, and I loved to have someone with experience help guide me through the complicating feelings I refused to discuss with anyone out in the real world. But the conversation kept getting more and more sexualised. I was young and inexperienced, and I thought it was interesting. And without knowing anything about this man, I thought I knew him well enough to trust him.

One day, he said he was going to drive through my hometown for work, and that he could come by before school so we could meet in real life. I told him that sounded like a good idea. He kept asking about when my parents were gone, and if I was entirely sure of their schedule. No alarm bells went off.

When he showed up, he was nothing like I imagined. He was old. The same age as my parents. And he was ugly. I thought it was obvious that we wouldn't do anything even though we had talked about having sex when we texted, and I also thought he cared about me. How wrong could I have been?

He raped me, and I completely froze. I covered my chest with my hands, and I just wanted him to finish and leave. He kept his sunglasses on the entire time, and he smelt like old cigarettes and peppermint.

He left after he finished. Picked up all his things and went out the door while I was lying still. After he left, he sent me a text. Something along the lines of "it couldn't have been that bad for you." I got dressed and went to school. There, I told one of the girls in my class that I had been raped. She didn't say much, and apparently thought it was weird that I had shared it with her. And I didn't dare to tell any adults in my life because I was too ashamed. I didn't want anyone to know what had happened or blame me for being stupid.

I didn't go to the police until several years later when I turned 18. I gave them his phone number and what I thought was his name. They spent 1.5 years not doing a lot except for sending a letter to my parents when I had told them not to. After that, I got another letter saying the case was closed because they couldn't find enough evidence to go to court. In the letter, they had written his name as well as mine.

I couldn't help myself and looked up his name and phone number. I got several hits. A lot of girls and women were writing about him. He was contacting younger girls trying to get them to meet him. He was also sending obscene texts to several others. Some of the girls wrote that he operated under different identities, of which one was the name he had given me. I think that was the first time I was able to understand that he had deliberately tried to fool me. He had set out from the beginning to make sure I didn't know who he was when we met. It wasn't just that I had misunderstood.

For the fact that I did misunderstand I still blame myself. If I had done some background research on the name and number, I could have found something warning me about him before I met him. It taught me a gruesome lesson that ruined my life for a long time. But anytime I went on dates as an adult, I would Google everything people told me to check if it was true. To the extent that I would check company filings or publicly available tax returns to make sure they were who they claimed to be. Surprisingly often, I found men who would lie about their age or marital status, and when I confronted them, they thought I was the weird one.

For me, it helped to create a rule saying that anyone who lied about anything, I would never meet. It didn't matter what it was. If they were lying about it, their intentions for meeting me weren't right.

But I still wish I had dared to talk more about it when I was young. Or that someone would explain what potential predators could do to trick you. I felt so grown up back then, but I was just a kid. In addition to being young, I was also naïve.

I was so used to having to pretend that everything felt natural that I didn't realise when I should have taken control of the situation. I had trouble setting proper boundaries because I had no idea what they were supposed to be. And I didn't want to be mean by imposing the wrong ones.

As for the man who raped me and most likely also several other young girls. He's still free, and he currently works with disabled people. Thinking about the damage he might still be inflicting onto others is killing me every day. But there's nothing more I can do.

When I reported the rape, the police officer was more concerned about asking me what type of underwear I had been wearing and how many sexual partners I had than to ask about what he did to me. One woman even accused me of being on drugs and lying because I didn't look her in the eyes while telling her about the rape.

This is now a very long time ago. But unfortunately, this system hasn't improved over the years, and I've seen several of my good friends become victims of rapes that were never taken seriously by the police. Rape isn't a punishable offence in Norway in practice, because the police will go out of their way to slut-shame the girl or just not prioritise the case. This again leads to most women not even daring to report sexual abuse and rape or trying to get help.

National reports show that as many as 1 in 10 women in Norway is raped while 1 in 4 is sexually assaulted in some form (Thoresen & Hjemdal, 2014). Of the women being raped, only 10.5% dare report it to the police (Thoresen & Hjemdal, 2014). The police again choose to not prosecute 83.7% of the cases (Huuse et al., 2018). Of the very few that reach the court system, 30% of the rapists are acquitted (Kripos, 2015). This leaves us with an astonishing 1.4% in all rapes leading to a conviction for the rapists. Can you blame me for being disillusioned?

Norway has been criticised by Amnesty International for not respecting human rights and failing to protect victims of sexual crimes. Amnesty has recommended that the Norwegian government changes the legislation and definition of rape, that it starts to set aside enough resources to the police and the prosecution, and that it funds support centres for survivors (Amnesty International, 2019). None of the recommendations is being followed.

I can only hope that it's better in other countries or that it will improve in the future. As for now, the only positive thing I'm taking with me from the experience is that I have the ability to understand and help others when they're going through the same thing.

Harassment at work

Women on the spectrum have a higher chance of being targeted by both familiar and unfamiliar predators in social settings. But we might also suffer the same type of abuse at work. Sometimes, that abuse isn't as serious as rape or other types of violence, but it can still be damaging.

Sometime before the #MeToo movement took off on Twitter, I experienced several uncomfortable incidents myself. I started out as an investment banker when I finished school. And like most jobs in finance, it's dominated by macho male behaviour and has a reputation for being toxic. I didn't think too much about it before I started because I believed the rumours were based on outdated information. I had seen so little to any of this behaviour at the school where I studied finance, so why would it suddenly become an issue now?

But the bank I worked for was still populated by the same sleazy older men that had always been there, and it didn't take long before I started noticing. I had traders making remarks about the way I looked when I was presenting something. At company events, both clients and colleagues would hit on me and ask for sex, and sometimes bosses would make jokes about me hooking up with clients to get a deal.

Not only did the older men disappoint me, but I also started seeing the same type of behaviour amongst guys I went to school with after they had only spent a couple of years in the firm. Lunches at work were frequently spent listening to guys my age making lists of who was supposed to sleep with the new interns first.

All of those things bothered me, and I started getting more and more tired of it. But it was one incident in particular that made me realise I wouldn't survive if I stayed in that hotbed of toxic masculinity.

A guy who was leading one of our international trading desks from New York, whom I had known since I started out as an intern, had come back to the Oslo office a few days before Christmas. I saw him at a club close to our office, and since we hadn't spoken in a while, I took a break from my friends to have a drink with him.

He then told me something very dramatic. He said there was going to be a restructuring of the company during the next quarter, and that there was a list with names of the people who were getting fired. Apparently, most of my bosses were on the list. So I was, of course, anxious and wanted to know more. And since I had worked with him several years earlier, I trusted him and came back to the apartment the bank rented for him after we had finished our drinks.

It turned out that everything he told me was true. Those people did leave the bank in a rather messy way a few months later. But what hadn't been true was his intention to discuss it with me and keeping it professional.

I told him clearly that I wasn't looking to flirt or have sex with him, and that I was only joining him so we could discuss it without the noisy club music. And he seemed to understand. But it didn't take long for him to try to physically attack me and hold me down. When I pushed him away and tried to leave, he blocked the entrance and grabbed my phone. Then he told me he would have me fired if I told anyone what happened.

I was mature enough to report it to my boss and the HR department right away, but they mostly looked the other way and said it was after working hours, so it wasn't their problem. Prompted by HR, the guy gave me an apology and said he didn't remember anything that had happened, but that didn't really help.

HR now seemed to think I was a difficult employee because I had reported this in addition to all the comments made by traders and colleagues. I even went as far as reporting it to the woman who was the bank's CEO in Norway at the time. Nothing changed. And a few months later, when several of my male colleagues got a raise and were asked not to tell me, I realised I had no future there.

I was disappointed in both them and myself. Myself because I had been fooled once again. The man who assaulted me because I believed he was a friend within the company who also viewed me the same way. But my biggest disappointment was with the bank and the HR department. I decided then and there I couldn't stay in such an environment and started sending out my CV to headhunters.

Within the next year, I left Oslo for London, and I've never looked back. Sometimes, taking care of yourself doesn't only mean that you need to read people and situations better, but you also need to take yourself out of environments where you'll be mistreated.

I was told at the bank that I came across as flirtatious and needed to take precautions at company events or not participate at all. Maybe it's true that I didn't understand the signals I was sending out when all I wanted was to be nice and likeable. But it still doesn't mean that any of those men had the right to treat me like that. I clearly said that I wasn't interested, and the people who won't respect that, are the worst kind you can ever encounter.

Long-term, I hope that work can be a place women will be respected. And I also hope that both men and women in more powerful positions will become more mindful of what type of pressure they put on others.

When a relationship turns abusive

Not only do women fear the actions of strangers. But we're also afraid of what our loved ones can do to us. And in many instances, those are the people who can hurt us the most. Not just emotionally, but physically as well.

When this happens in a relationship, it can be a lot harder to understand, and it can be more difficult to get away from. Because this person most likely just a few weeks ago acted like a loving and caring partner who said they would do anything for you. If someone turns abusive in a relationship, it often doesn't happen right away, and the feelings you had for them in the beginning don't automatically disappear.

I've experienced several versions of toxic relationships when I was younger. One was in the category above. He started out as the man of my dreams. The love I felt for him was intense, and I was convinced that this was something very special. We quickly moved in together, and that's when he started to change.

What I first noticed was snide remarks about other women. It could be his ex-girlfriends or women he just noticed on the street. He would call them slutty or ugly, and if I said anything, he would say that he was just joking.

Then he started turning those comments towards me. And they weren't jokes anymore. He thought I was a whore who should be ashamed of my sexual past, although I had fewer sexual partners than him. If I went out, he would say that I was dressed like a hooker and that he couldn't trust me if I chose to look like that.

It turned even worse when he tried stopping me from spending time with friends. And he could scream for hours if I didn't stay at home with him. He also told me I needed to quit my job to spend more time taking care of him and the home. He said I was a bad girlfriend for not wanting to iron his shirts and cook him dinner every day, and he made jokes about using cameras, GPS trackers and microphones to spy on me.

When he started to show violent tendencies, I had enough. The pressure he had me under, felt like a slow-cooking stew that I hadn't noticed because the heat got turned up so slowly. When I saw him crush an entire bed to pieces right in front of me because he was angry, I vowed to get away from him as soon as possible.

The next time I encountered a boyfriend who started making the same comments about women and also joked about controlling where I was, I left the minute he started. The red flags were now firmly planted in my mind because I had suffered the consequences of not noticing them before.

I talk now as if that was the first time I was with someone who showed violent tendencies, but that's also not the case. In my first marriage, my ex-husband would often try to hold me so I couldn't leave the room while we were having an argument. And at one point, he also put his hands around my throat and over my mouth. I didn't properly react to that as an act of violence at the time, but I should have. Controlling you physically during an argument, unless you're about to harm yourself or others, is never ok.

I'm very lucky that the man I'm married to now is nothing like this, and I'm older and wiser than I was back then. He's the complete opposite of those men, and shows me the compassion and respect you should expect from someone who loves you. But getting me from there to here took a lot of conscious work.

To cope, I now have rules for things I don't like in people, and I try to stick to them. It also means I sometimes overreact if someone does something similar that isn't that bad. But I think it's better to lean this way than the other.

I can't be with someone who lies to me. But I've adjusted this a few times because making a mistake when telling me about a minor detail and getting this wrong, might not mean that the person intended to lie.

Anyone who makes negative comments about women in general or women they've dated are off my list. If they can say things like that about others, they will certainly not stand up for you in the future.

If someone talks negatively behind my back, I don't care how much I would have liked to be friends with that person. Comments like that are hurtful, and I don't want to risk being hurt even more the next time it happens.

If I'm not genuinely looking for something that's purely sexual, I don't meet with people who are alluding to the fact that they want to sleep with me before we've met. Also, if someone doesn't have any shared interests with me, I don't waste time on them, hoping that they will develop those.

If someone tries to pressure me into doing something I don't want to, not only do I not do it, but that person isn't someone I want to have in my life. An example of that was a very high profile London lawyer who tried to pressure me into coming home with him by first putting his own address in the uber instead of mine, and then getting angry when I said I would order another car because I didn't feel comfortable "just having a glass of wine" upstairs.

Common expressions like "it's just a coffee," I have now

filed under sexual invitations. The same goes for having a drink alone with men I meet at work. I've believed people too many times when they invited me for that, so I don't take that risk anymore.

Self-work

The most important thing you can do for yourself after this chapter is to spend some time defining your boundaries. If you write down explicit rules, that can help you become more aware when someone does something you're not comfortable with.

It doesn't mean that I think women are responsible for what violent partners or strangers do to them. That will only be on them, and them alone. But we all have different boundaries and different things we're ok with. And it can be useful to know what yours are so you can quickly point it out if you're in a situation where something uncomfortable happens.

Take some time now to write down your rules. Something to help you get going is to think about uncomfortable situations in the past.

Define your boundaries:
1. When do you want to meet someone in real life that you've only spoken with on a dating site or app?
2. What information do you need to have before you agree to meet them?
3. What places are you comfortable meeting?
4. When do you want to end the date?
5. Are you comfortable drinking alcohol and how much?
6. Do you want to do drugs, and in case you do, which people would you like to have around you as you do that?

7. What is the difference for you between a friend and a romantic interest?
8. When do you want to tell someone that you have feelings for them?
9. Which things would you not accept when dating someone casually?
10. What would you not accept when dating someone exclusively?
11. What would you not accept in a long-term relationship or when getting married to someone?
12. How many times must you tell someone that you're uncomfortable before you leave?
13. How much time would you like to spend with someone you're dating?
14. Which things are you not willing to change about yourself?
15. What type of touching are you not comfortable with, and when do you feel that someone is getting into your personal space?
16. What types of comments are you not willing to accept about yourself or others?
17. What type of work events are you comfortable with?
18. What type of criticism do you find constructive, and what will just put you down?
19. Which things would you cut out of your life to please a partner, and which would you always want to keep?
20. What type of language do you accept when someone is talking about past relationships or other women in general?

Getting diagnosed

How to get a diagnosis

Women are often under-diagnosed when it comes to autism. And all the studies I've used for this book seem to estimate that there are several times more men than women on the spectrum. But most people now believe that these numbers aren't realistic. And there are several reasons why women tend to either be diagnosed late or not at all.

As mentioned in the second chapter, most research and diagnostic criteria are based on findings amongst boys and men. Women don't always have the same special interests and they can often seem like they master social situations well. This is especially true for women who don't have any learning disabilities and have average or high intelligence.

They tend to mask their symptoms by copying other women and analysing every social situation to figure out what the acceptable responses are. These women are rarely diagnosed as kids. They're doing so well in school, and even though they might be a bit odd, they're not noticed by parents or teachers. When they get older, they often get other symptoms. They can be depressed or become physically exhausted after using so much energy on trying to "act normal."

For these women, getting a diagnosis is often challenging. Most specialists work with children, and trying to diagnose an adult is inherently different. The person making the diagnosis also needs to be familiar with how the symptoms present in women, and most professionals simply don't inhibit this knowledge.

Psychiatrists in different countries have different guidelines and diagnostic criteria, but they're mostly overlapping. For example, you can see both the DSM-5 criteria and the ICD-11 criteria being used in the same country. But the person diagnosing has the flexibility to choose what they want to use, and to exercise their best judgement.

To make a diagnosis, enough information about the person's behaviour must be gathered to see if all the necessary criteria are met. There are several ways to do this, but the most common is to interview the person being diagnosed along with a parent or another informant.

These interviews often try to set up situations between the person diagnosing and the person who is suspected to be on the spectrum so their reactions can be observed. One such interview style is called the Autism Diagnostic Observation Schedule (ADOS) and another which is done with a caregiver or other observant is the Autism Diagnostic Interview-Revised (ADI-R). There are several other interview styles like the Diagnostic Interview for Social and Communication Disorders (DISCO), but these are considered the most accurate and are widely used.

Normally, you'll either meet with a psychiatrist or someone

who is specifically trained in autism assessment. Often a normal therapist isn't qualified to make an official diagnosis. You'll also usually need to find someone who specialises in diagnosing adults, and who has experience with diagnosing women.

Using public healthcare to get diagnosed as an adult woman can be challenging. We're not highly prioritised, and waiting times can be several years from getting a referral to being diagnosed. If you want to go down that road, you should start by speaking to your regular doctor.

He or she is not likely to have more than basic knowledge about autism, so you need to be prepared when discussing with them. It helps if you have some examples in each category of the diagnostic criteria. Your doctor can also ask you to fill out a form like the AQ-10 so he or she can do an initial screening before referring you to a specialist.

For my first chat with my GP (short for General Practitioner in the UK), I told him I had read a lot about autism and felt like most of the descriptions resonated with me. I also told him it would explain most of my odd childhood behaviour. Since autism is with you your entire life, it's important to be able to track some of your difficulties to childhood as well as present time.

The doctor will also usually ask you for your motivation for getting a diagnosis, and you should be prepared with a response. They want you to acknowledge that your life won't suddenly change just because you're officially diagnosed. As part of this chapter, I've written about the advantages of getting an official diagnosis, so feel free to see which reasons apply to you and share those with your doctor.

If you never had a therapist who told you that you have symptoms of autism, the doctor will potentially also ask why you started suspecting that you're on the spectrum. You can tell them you've always known you were different but were unaware of how autism looks like in women. You can also refer to books you've read about the subject and tell them that it explains things you've struggled with.

Sometimes, the doctor will be helpful and make a referral. But I've heard of countless of people having bad experiences where the doctor is difficult, and either doesn't understand the person's need to get a diagnosis or are misinformed about how autism presents in women.

Some say that since you're able to have a two-way conversation with them you can't possibly be on the spectrum. If you don't have issues with eye contact, this is also something doctors seem to comment on. Some have also said that if you're self-aware enough to seek out a diagnosis, you're not on the spectrum. If any of these things happen to you, remember that this doctor isn't the specialist and keep pushing by showing him test results and explain how autism is different for women. All you need is for them to make a referral somewhere else.

Sometimes, you end up meeting the same type of prejudices from the person who is expected to diagnose you. Appointments can be short, meaning you don't have time to look deeper into masking or how the symptoms work for you. Make sure you do some research on clinics in your area so you know the person you're meeting is capable of diagnosing adult women. You can ask your doctor to refer you specifically to one of them.

I see women sharing their frustration from unsuccessful diagnostic assessments almost every day. They often score way above the threshold on standardised questionnaires, but the diagnostician refuses to make a final diagnosis because they're too "high-functioning." Sometimes, the specialists even think they're doing women a favour by not labelling them as autistic.

This is a very difficult issue, as most of us want to be on our best behaviour when we interact with someone who can get us a diagnosis. And if the interview only lasts for an hour, many of us can use strategies to compensate and seem neurotypical, even though we can have plenty of real-life examples of what happens when we're not masking.

If you don't get a diagnosis the first time, you can go back to your doctor and ask him or her to refer you somewhere else, but you can also choose to go private so you can find a clinic with the right expertise.

All of these stories, plus the insanely long waiting list, made me look up a private clinic. I made sure it was a clinic where they had experience with diagnosing adult women and sent several emails back and forth with one of the people who were going to assess me before booking the appointment.

Some people are lucky and get a private assessment covered by their health insurance, but it doesn't seem to be standard to include for adults. If you're comfortable reaching out to your insurance to discuss it, I definitely would, as a private assessment can cost several thousand pounds.

The assessment day

When you get a referral for an assessment, it can be helpful to know what to expect.

Before I went to mine, I had several forms to fill out. They were different from the standardised AQ-10 and AQ-50. They were also different from what I've seen other women fill out before their appointments, so the information you need to provide seems to differ from clinic to clinic.

The forms included questions about social contact, employment history and education, along with lists of developmental questions from childhood. A large part also covered sensory issues, which for some women can be the most difficult part of being on the spectrum.

On the day, they had asked me to bring an informant with me. The preference would have been to have a parent or someone who knew me well as a child, but this wasn't possible, so my husband came with me instead. Two doctors had set aside three hours to speak with both me and my husband. The diagnosis itself was made after a long interview following a specific structure to cover all symptoms of autism.

Some of the questions are straightforward, and you're asked to give examples from your adult life and childhood. But they also try to see how you're able to interact with them during the assessment. When we were discussing special interests, one of the doctors asked me to talk a bit about wine. She then commented that her husband was also very much into wine and that he had a fridge for storage. I asked her what type of fridge it was and wanted to know about sound vibrations and technical details. She said she didn't know, but that it was very interesting that this was the thing I chose to follow up on. Not that she had a husband.

We also discussed early development in terms of language. They asked me about my first words, which were, in fact, not mum or dad, but "horse." It's a story my parents love to tell because it's unusual for a child to connect with other things than their parents first. It turned out that this was probably a part of my autism, and it was something I didn't know.

I also told them how I always knew that I was different as a kid without being able to recognise how. I just knew that I didn't fit in with my peers and that I didn't have the same interests as them. They told me that this was fairly normal for someone on the spectrum to experience, but that I should be able to have great relationships with people as an adult with the right tools. The social isolation one feels when being different as a child can be a heavy burden to bear, but to understand that it doesn't have to be that way is an equally welcome relief.

I've carried a lot of shame from incidents early on in life where I would insult other kids or make them cry, but the process of getting a diagnosis made me understand that it wasn't something I could help back then. And hearing it framed by someone who is a specialist on autism was very helpful.

We spent some time on sensory issues, and they recommended that I go and see an occupational therapist who specialises in autism and sensory integration. They told me that I needed to slow down and take care of my sensory needs and cut down on the time I spent socialising. And they provided me with very concrete tips on how to take control of that part of my life.

We also discussed my romantic relationships over the years and if I ever felt close to other people. I told them I had a few people in my life that I was very close with, and that most of them were neurodiverse in some way. At the end of the conversation, my husband was invited into the room as well, and they would ask him about his view of me in everyday situations, for example when my routine was interrupted, or how easy it was for me to have empathy for him.

The last hour of the appointment, I started getting a headache, and when I was done, I went home and slept for the rest of the day because I was so exhausted. But all in all, it was a very positive experience, and I'm glad I did it.

They already told me in the room that it was clear to them that I was autistic, but that isn't always the case. The official report came a month later, and it contained all the details we had discussed along with their assessment.

Self-diagnosing

My diagnostic process was mainly positive, and I'm happy

that I went through with it. But for some women, getting a diagnosis as an adult is either not possible or not something they want to pursue. Unfortunately, I see many people making judgemental comments towards those who choose to self-diagnose. But there are several legitimate reasons why someone would prefer this instead of getting an official diagnosis.

First of all, it can be very expensive to get a diagnosis as an adult. If insurance doesn't cover it, and you can't find anyone with the proper knowledge through government-paid healthcare, you might not be able to afford it. Going to a clinic can also involve expensive travelling and other logistical issues.

Some people also prefer to not have a diagnosis in writing anywhere because they're afraid it will affect their ability to get insurance, or that it will somehow be used against them in other areas of life. And as much as we wish the world was different, this can happen, and I understand that some people hesitate to get a diagnosis because they're worried about this.

Others are afraid of being judged by friends and family and want to keep it private. Unfortunately, there can be a stigma related to having an autism diagnosis. Personally, I don't think so, but I know of people who live in communities where this is the case, and although we can encourage everyone to get a formal diagnosis if they want one, I respect their choice to not do so if that makes them more comfortable.

Some women aren't willing to go through a process that can be stressful and not end in an official diagnosis because the doctors they meet don't take them seriously. With all the horror stories I've heard, I can understand that people feel that way.

Sometimes those stories also include women coming back from an assessment with a different diagnosis that they don't feel fit them. Some women are misdiagnosed with for example PTSD, mood disorders or borderline personality disorder, and it's understandable that people don't want to risk getting a label they don't think is correct.

They might also not feel the need for an official diagnosis, and if they're happy without having that official label, they can still be a part of the autistic community through support groups or by reading literature. Most people won't claim that your diagnosis is invalid just because you don't have the official paperwork.

Others are self-diagnosing while they're waiting for an assessment. Since this can take a long time, it would be pretty frustrating for those people to feel they weren't allowed to participate in autistic support communities or use the label on themselves for years while they're waiting for an appointment.

Ultimately, it's your decision if you want to seek a professional diagnosis or not. But you should know that even without one, you can get the benefits from just knowing about your autism and understanding which coping strategies and strengths come along with being on the spectrum.

Reasons to get a diagnosis

Advantages of having an official diagnosis can be many as well. For some people, getting the acknowledgement that this is the correct diagnosis for them can be important. It can make them accept and understand parts of them that have given them issues previously. It can provide them with a better understanding of how to approach work, social functions, and how to advocate for themselves.

Some women diagnosed late have said they felt a more positive sense of self after being diagnosed, and that they felt a greater sense of belonging when they had an autistic community to be a part of (Bargiela et al., 2016).

Sometimes, you'll also need an official diagnosis to get an

employer or a school to make adjustments for you. And you can also need a diagnosis to be able to get help and support from public healthcare. If you're unemployed, the diagnosis can be necessary for you to claim benefits from the government, or for you to be able to participate in support groups attempted at helping people on the spectrum getting job experience.

If you need to ask for facilitation when you travel or do other daily activities, it can also make you more confident stating that you're on the spectrum if you're backed by an official diagnosis.

Family, friends or partners can sometimes also be sceptical to our new diagnosis, and you could want one that's made by a professional to "prove" to them that autism isn't just something you're making up. It's sad that this is the case for many, but I know from my own experience that family might not believe you without having an official assessment first.

But ultimately, the greatest benefit is getting to know yourself and being able to see the issues you've had throughout your life in a new light. It can also give you a great start to work on problems you have in friendships or romantic relationships. It can give you a new way of exploring and understanding your strengths, as autism isn't just a fixed set of things that are wrong with us, but an uneven set of abilities where we often are just as strong or stronger as someone without autism.

Self-work

The self-work portion of this chapter is only necessary if you want to pursue an official diagnosis. It's only meant as a helping hand, and it's not a strict list of what you have to do to get diagnosed as every clinic will have their own requirements and ask you to fill out separate paperwork.

Prepare for the diagnostic assessment:

1. Search for Autism Spectrum Quotient tests and fill out the one that consists of 50 questions and is called the AQ-50. You can show the results to your doctor when you ask for a referral.
2. Write a list of concrete examples of when you've experienced symptoms of autism consistent with ICD-11 or DSM-5. Make sure to include examples from childhood as well as adulthood. The complete criteria can easily be found through a Google search.
3. You can also assemble your self-work questions from this book, as we have covered most of the topics you'll discuss during a diagnostic assessment. Make sure to include your examples of the following:
    1. Social difficulties including trouble with body language, conversations, emotional understanding and relationships
    2. Need for routines and sameness
    3. Sensory issues
    4. Stimming
    5. Meltdowns
    6. Trouble with executive functioning
    7. Special interests
    8. Co-morbidities
4. Write down why you think you would benefit from getting an official diagnosis as doctors will often want to know your reasoning before they refer you for an assessment. You can use examples from this chapter if you can't think of anything specific for yourself.
5. Research clinics in your area that specialise in assessing autism in adult women. Don't expect that your doctor will know about these already. Then book an appointment with your regular doctor to get a referral. If

you want to do the assessment privately, you can often contact the clinic directly.

Superpowers

What are our superpowers?

Do we actually have superpowers? Or are we desperately grasping for something that isn't there? I don't think it's right to measure neurotypicals against autistic people to say that one is always better. And the same way all neurotypicals are different, all autistic people are also different from each other.

It's clear to me that we live in a neurotypical world where only a few of us are lucky enough to be in an environment that fully cater to our different sets of needs. This means that much of what we do and experience is measured against the neurotypical standard. And that's what I want to get away from. When we're measured against someone who has a completely different starting point than us, we can't help but feel like a failure.

But we're not. As you have seen throughout the book, there

are many ways an autistic person can seem stronger than someone who isn't on the spectrum. But we also have things we struggle with, and I think that it's equally ignorant to pretend that those things don't exist.

And when we struggle, we should get help. Not so we can change the way we act to pretend like we're neurotypicals, but to be able to live in the world without being judged and bothered by for example unpleasant sensory input.

I wanted to write this book so that more people than me could try to see autism not only as a weakness but also as a strength. Women are so often judged when they don't follow social norms. But our differences can help us see things in a completely new way, and what we do can change other people's lives. We can invent things. We can have a new take on research and technology. And we can see the details that no one else can. With our intense passion, we can also bring our ideas to life.

Let us stay in touch

I hope that reading this book gave you something of value. If it was understanding autism better, feeling like you and I have something in common, accepting yourself, or motivating you to learn more.

If you want to stay in touch with me or get updated when I publish new books or articles, you can register for my newsletter at christinelion.com.

And if you enjoyed what you read, I would be grateful if you would leave a review at amazon.

Bibliography

Abrahams, B. S., & Geschwind, D. H. (2008). Advances in autism genetics: On the threshold of a new neurobiology. *Nature Reviews. Genetics,* 9(5), 341–355. https://doi.org/10.1038/nrg2346

Alvares, G. A., Bebbington, K., Cleary, D., Evans, K., Glasson, E. J., Maybery, M. T., ... Whitehouse, A. J. (2019). The misnomer of 'high-functioning autism': Intelligence is an imprecise predictor of functional abilities at diagnosis. *Autism.* https://doi.org/10.1177/1362361319852831

Amnesty International. (2019). Time for change: Justice for rape survivors in the Nordic countries. https://www.amnesty.org/en/documents/eur01/0089/2019/en/

Anthony, L. G., Kenworthy, L., Yerys, B. E., Jankowski, K. F.,

James, J. D., Harms, M. B., ... Wallace, G. L. (2013). Interests in high-functioning autism are more intense, interfering, and idiosyncratic, but not more circumscribed, than those in neurotypical development. *Development and Psychopathology*, 25(3), 643–652. https://doi.org/10.1017/S0954579413000072

Attwood, T. (2006). *The Complete Guide to Asperger's Syndrome [kindle format]*. Retrieved from https://www.amazon.co.uk/gp/product/B0050IY61G/ref=kinw_myk_ro_title

Baio, J. (2018). Prevalence of Autism Spectrum Disorder Among Children Aged 8 Years—Autism and Developmental Disabilities Monitoring Network, 11 Sites, United States, 2014. *MMWR. Surveillance Summaries*, 67. https://doi.org/10.15585/mmwr.ss6706a1

Bargiela, S., Steward, R., & Mandy, W. (2016). The Experiences of Late-diagnosed Women with Autism Spectrum Conditions: An Investigation of the Female Autism Phenotype. *Journal of Autism and Developmental Disorders*, 46(10), 3281–3294. https://doi.org/10.1007/s10803-016-2872-8

Baron-Cohen, S. (2009). Autism: The Empathizing-Systemizing (E-S) Theory. *Annals of the New York Academy of Sciences*, 1156(1), 68–80. https://doi.org/10.1111/j.1749-6632.2009.04467.x

Baron-cohen, S., Bolton, P., Wheelwright, S., Scahill, V., Short, L., Mead, G., & Smith, A. (1998). Autism occurs more often in families of physicists, engineers, and mathematicians.

Autism, 296–301.

Baron-Cohen, S., Johnson, D., Asher, J., Wheelwright, S., Fisher, S. E., Gregersen, P. K., & Allison, C. (2013). Is synaesthesia more common in autism? *Molecular Autism*. https://doi.org/10.1186/2040-2392-4-40

Baron-Cohen & Wheelwright, S. (2004). The Empathy Quotient: An Investigation of Adults with Asperger Syndrome or High Functioning Autism, and Normal Sex Differences. *Journal of Autism and Developmental Disorders*, Vol. 34, No. 2. https://www.researchgate.net/profile/Simon_Baron-Cohen/publication/8543379_The_Empathy_Quotient_An_Investigation_of_Adults_With_Asperger_Syndrome_or_High_Functioning_Autism_and_Normal_Sex_Differences/links/00b7d5140af309ef7d000000/The-Empathy-Quotient-An-Investigation-of-Adults-With-Asperger-Syndrome-or-High-Functioning-Autism-and-Normal-Sex-Differences.pdf

Bebbington, P., Brugha, T., Coid, J., Crawford, M., Deverill, C., D'Souza, J., Doyle, M., Farrell, M., Fuller, E., Jenkins, R., Jotangia, D., Harris, J., Hussey, D., King, M., McManus, S., Meltzer, H., Nicholson, S., Palmer, B., Pickup, D., Purdon, S., Sadler, K., Scholes, S., Smith, J., Thompson, J., Tyrer, P., Wardle, H., Weich, S., & Wessely, S. (2009). Autism Spectrum Disorders in adults living in households throughout England Report from the Adult Psychiatric Morbidity Survey 2007. https://digital.nhs.uk/data-and-information/publications/

statistical/autism-spectrum-disorders-in-adults-living-in-households-throughout-england/autism-spectrum-disorders-in-adults-living-in-households-throughout-england-2007-report-from-the-adult-psychiatric-morbidity-survey

Begeer, S., Mandell, S., Wijnker-Holmes, B., Venderbosch, S., Rem, D., Stekelenburg, F., & Koot, H. M. (2013). Sex differences in the timing of identification among children and adults with autism spectrum disorders. *Journal of Autism and Developmental Disorders, 43*(5), 1151-1160. https://doi.org/10.1007/s10803-012-1656-z

Ben-Sasson, A., Hen, L., Fluss, R., Cermak, S. A., Engel-Yeger, B., & Gal, E. (2009). A Meta-Analysis of Sensory Modulation Symptoms in Individuals with Autism Spectrum Disorders. *Journal of Autism and Developmental Disorders, 39*(1), 1–11. https://doi.org/10.1007/s10803-008-0593-3

Bogdashina, O. (2016). *Sensory Perceptual Issues in Autism and Asperger Syndrome, Second Edition: Different Sensory Experiences - Different Perceptual Worlds*. Jessica Kingsley Publishers.

Bonnel, A., McAdams, S., Smith, B., Berthiaume, C., Bertone, A., Ciocca, V., ... Mottron, L. (2010). Enhanced pure-tone pitch discrimination among persons with autism but not Asperger syndrome. *Neuropsychologia, 48*(9), 2465–2475. https://doi.org/10.1016/j.neuropsychologia.2010.04.020

Cain, S. (2012). Quiet [kindle format]. Retrieved from https://www.amazon.co.uk/gp/product/B0074YVW1G/ref=kinw_myk_ro_title

Cappadocia, M.C., Weiss, J.A. & Pepler, D. (2012). Bullying Experiences Among Children and Youth with Autism Spectrum Disorders. *Journal of Autism and Devevelopmental Disorders* 42: 266. https://doi.org/10.1007/s10803-011-1241-x

Case-Smith, J., Weaver, L. L., & Fristad, M. A. (2015). A systematic review of sensory processing interventions for children with autism spectrum disorders. *Autism*, 19(2), 133–148. https://doi.org/10.1177/1362361313517762

Cassidy, S., Bradley, P., Robinson, J., Allison, C., McHugh, M., & Baron-Cohen, B. Suicidal ideation and suicide plans or attempts in adults with Asperger's syndrome attending a specialist diagnostic clinic: a clinical cohort study. *The Lancet Psychiatry*, Volume 1, Issue 2, 142-147. https://doi.org/10.1016/S2215-0366(14)70248-2

Chaidez, V., Hansen, R. L., & Hertz-Picciotto, I. (2014). Gastrointestinal problems in children with autism, developmental delays or typical development. *Journal of Autism and Developmental Disorders*, 44(5), 1117–1127. https://doi.org/10.1007/s10803-013-1973-x

Crespi, B. J. (2016). Autism As a Disorder of High Intelligence. *Frontiers in Neuroscience, 10.* https://doi.org/10.3389/fnins.2016.00300

Cridland, E. K., Jones, S. C., Caputi, P. & Magee, C. A. (2014). Being a girl in a boys' world: Investigating the experiences of girls with autism spectrum disorders during adolescence. *Journal of Autism and Developmental Disorders*, 44 (6), 1261-1274. https://doi.org/10.1007/

s10803-013-1985-6

Dean, M., Harwood, R., & Kasari, C. (2017). The art of camouflage: Gender differences in the social behaviours of girls and boys with autism spectrum disorder. Retrieved 19 August 2019, from http://library.autism.org.uk/Portal/Default/en-GB/RecordView/Index/45876

Demetriou, E. A., Lampit, A., Quintana, D. S., Naismith, S. L., Song, Y. J. C., Pye, J. E., ... Guastella, A. J. (2018). Autism spectrum disorders: A meta-analysis of executive function. *Molecular Psychiatry*, 23(5), 1198–1204. https://doi.org/10.1038/mp.2017.75

Duhigg, C. (2012). *The Power of Habit: Why We Do What We Do, and How to Change [kindle format]* (19th ed). Retrieved from https://www.amazon.co.uk/Power-Habit-Why-What-Change-ebook/dp/B006WAIV6M/ref=tmm_kin_swatch_0?_encoding=UTF8&qid=1564536035&sr=8-1

Dworzynski, K., Ronald, A., Bolton, P., & Happé F. (2012). How Different Are Girls and Boys Above and Below the Diagnostic Threshold for Autism Spectrum Disorders? *Journal of the American Academy of Child & Adolescent Psychiatry*, Volume 51, Issue 8, 788-797. https://doi.org/10.1016/j.jaac.2012.05.018

Eccles, J., Iodice, V., Dowell, N., Owens, A., Hughes, L., Skipper, S., ... Critchley, H. (2014). Joint hyper mobility and autonomic hyperactivity: relevance to neurodevelopmental disorders. *Journal of Neurology,*

Neurosurgery & Psychiatry, 85(8), e3. https://doi.org/10.1136/jnnp-2014-308883.9

Ferriss, T. (2011). *The 4-Hour Body: An Uncommon Guide to Rapid Fat-loss, Incredible Sex and Becoming Superhuman [kindle format]*. Retrieved from https://www.amazon.co.uk/4-Hour-Body-Uncommon-Incredible-Superhuman-ebook/dp/B004M8S3Y6/ref=tmm_kin_swatch_0?_encoding=UTF8&qid=1564535894&sr=8-1

Fournier, K. A., Hass, C. J., Naik, S. K., Lodha, N., & Cauraugh, J. H. (2010). Motor Coordination in Autism Spectrum Disorders: A Synthesis and Meta-Analysis. *Journal of Autism and Developmental Disorders, 40*(10), 1227–1240. https://doi.org/10.1007/s10803-010-0981-3

George, R., & Stokes, M. A. (2018). Sexual Orientation in Autism Spectrum Disorder. *Autism Research, 11*(1), 133–141. https://doi.org/10.1002/aur.1892

Goh, S., & Peterson, B. S. (2012). Imaging evidence for disturbances in multiple learning and memory systems in persons with autism spectrum disorders. *Developmental Medicine & Child Neurology, 54*(3), 208–213. https://doi.org/10.1111/j.1469-8749.2011.04153.x

Goyal, M., Singh, S., Sibinga, E. M. S., Gould, N. F., Rowland-Seymour, A., Sharma, R., … Haythornthwaite, J. A. (2014). Meditation Programs for Psychological Stress and Well-being: A Systematic Review and Meta-analysis. *JAMA Internal Medicine, 174*(3), 357–368. https://doi.org/10.1001/jamainternmed.2013.13018

Grandin, T. (2006). *Thinking in pictures [kindle format]*. Retrieved from https://www.amazon.co.uk/gp/product/ B00394UCLQ/ref=kinw_myk_ro_title

Hagenaars, S. P., Harris, S. E., Davies, G., Hill, W. D., Liewald, D. C. M., Ritchie, S. J., … Deary, I. J. (2016). Shared genetic aetiology between cognitive functions and physical and mental health in UK Biobank (*N*=112 151) and 24 GWAS consortia. *Molecular Psychiatry*, 21(11), 1624–1632. https://doi.org/10.1038/mp.2015.225

Happé, F., & Frith, U. (2006). The Weak Coherence Account: Detail-focused Cognitive Style in Autism Spectrum Disorders. *Journal of Autism and Developmental Disorders*, 36(1), 5–25. https://doi.org/10.1007/s10803-005-0039-0

Heaton, P. (2003). Pitch memory, labelling and disembedding in autism. *Journal of Child Psychology and Psychiatry.* https://doi.org/10.1111/1469-7610.00143

Hedley, D., & Uljarević, M. (2018). Systematic Review of Suicide in Autism Spectrum Disorder: Current Trends and Implications. *Curr Dev Disord Rep 5,* 65–76. https://doi.org/10.1007/s40474-018-0133-6

Heilman, M. E.,Wallen, A. S.,Fuchs, D.,Tamkins, M. M. (2004). Penalties for Success: Reactions to Women Who Succeed at Male Gender-Typed Tasks. *Journal of Applied Psychology,* Vol 89(3), 416-427. https://doi.org/10.1037/0021-9010.89.3.416

Heller, S. (2014). *Too loud, too bright, too fast, too tight: what to do if you are sensory defensive in an overstimulating world.* Retrieved from https://www.amazon.co.uk/gp/product/B00KVIBX98/ref=kinw_myk_ro_title

Hill, E. L. (2004). Executive dysfunction in autism. *Trends in Cognitive Sciences*, 8(1), 26–32. https://doi.org/10.1016/j.tics.2003.11.003

Hirvikoski, T., Mittendorfer-Rutz, E., Boman, M., Larsson, H., Lichtenstein, P., & Bölte, S. (2016). Premature mortality in autism spectrum disorder. *British Journal of Psychiatry*, 208(3), 232-238. doi:10.1192/bjp.bp.114.160192

Hofmann, S. G., Sawyer, A. T., Witt, A. A., & Oh, D. (2010). The Effect of Mindfulness-Based Therapy on Anxiety and Depression: A Meta-Analytic Review. *Journal of Consulting and Clinical Psychology*, 78(2), 169–183. https://doi.org/10.1037/a0018555

Howlin, P., Goode, S., Hutton, J., & Rutter, M. (2009). Savant skills in autism: Psychometric approaches and parental reports. *Philosophical Transactions of the Royal Society B: Biological Sciences*, 364(1522), 1359–1367. https://doi.org/10.1098/rstb.2008.0328

Huke, V., Turk, J., Saeidi, S., Kent, A., & Morgan, J. F. (2013). Autism Spectrum Disorders in Eating Disorder Populations: A Systematic Review. *European Eating Disorders Review*, 21(5), 345–351. https://doi.org/10.1002/erv.2244

Hull, L., Petrides, K.V., Allison, C., Smith, P., Baron-Cohen, S., Lai, M., & Mandy, W. (2017) "Putting on My Best Normal": Social Camouflaging in Adults with Autism Spectrum Conditions. *Journal of Autism and Developmental Disorders*, 47: 2519. https://doi.org/10.1007/s10803-017-3166-5

Huuse, C., Nærø, A., Bakken, J. & Nilsen, S. (2018). *Verdens Gang.* https://www.vg.no/spesial/2018/voldtektstall/?utm_source=vgfront&utm_content=row-1

James, L. (2017). *Odd Girl Out: An Autistic Woman in a Neurotypical World [kindle format]* (Main market ed). Retrieved from https://www.amazon.co.uk/gp/product/B01LVXOWRK/ref=kinw_myk_ro_title

Jolliffe, T., & Baron-Cohen, S. (1997). Are People with Autism and Asperger Syndrome Faster Than Normal on the Embedded Figures Test? *Journal of Child Psychology and Psychiatry*, 38(5), 527–534. https://doi.org/10.1111/j.1469-7610.1997.tb01539.x

Jones, C. R. G., Happé, F., Baird, G., Simonoff, E., Marsden, A. J. S., Tregay, J., ... Charman, T. (2009). Auditory discrimination and auditory sensory behaviours in autism spectrum disorders. *Neuropsychologia, 47*(13), 2850–2858. https://doi.org/10.1016/j.neuropsychologia.2009.06.015

Kimball, J. G., Lynch, K. M., Stewart, K. C., Williams, N. E., Thomas, M. A., & Atwood, K. D. (2007). Using Salivary Cortisol to Measure the Effects of a Wilbarger Protocol–Based Procedure on Sympathetic Arousal: A Pilot Study. *American Journal of Occupational Therapy,* 61(4), 406–413. https://doi.org/10.5014/ajot.61.4.406

Kirkovski, M., Enticott, P.G. & Fitzgerald, P.B. (2013). A Review of the Role of Female Gender in Autism Spectrum Disorders. *Journal of Autism & Developmental Disorders,* 43: 2584. https://doi.org/10.1007/s10803-013-1811-1

Klin, A., Danovitch, J. H., Merz, A. B., & Volkmar, F. R. (2007). Circumscribed Interests in Higher Functioning Individuals with Autism Spectrum Disorders: An Exploratory Study. *Research and Practice for Persons with Severe Disabilities*, 32(2), 89–100. https://doi.org/10.2511/rpsd.32.2.89

Knickmayer, R. C., Wheelwright, S., Baron-Cohen, S. B. (2007). Sex-typical Play: Masculinization/Defeminization in Girls with an Autism Spectrum Condition. *Journal of Autism and Developmental Disorders*. https://doi.org/10.1007/s10803-007-0475-0

Kohane, I. S., McMurry, A., Weber, G., MacFadden, D., Rappaport, L., Kunkel, L., … Churchill, S. (2012). The Co-Morbidity Burden of Children and Young Adults with Autism Spectrum Disorders. https://doi.org/10.1371/journal.pone.0033224

Kondo, M. (2014). The life-changing magic of tidying: a simple, effective way to banish clutter forever.

Kripos. (2015). Voldtektssituasjonen 2014. https://www.politiet.no/globalassets/04-aktuelt-tall-og-fakta/voldtekt-og-seksuallovbrudd/voldtektssituasjonen-i-norge-2014.pdf

Krumm, N., O'Roak, B. J., Shendure, J., & Eichler, E. E. (2014). A de novo convergence of autism genetics and molecular neuroscience. *Trends in Neurosciences*, 37(2), 95–105. https://doi.org/10.1016/j.tins.2013.11.005

Lai, M., Lombardo, M. V., Ruigrok A., Chakrabarti, B., Auyeung, B., Szatmari, P., Happé F., Baron-Cohen, S., & MRC AIMS

Consortium. (2016). Quantifying and exploring camouflaging in men and women with autism. *Autism*, Vol. 21(6), 690–702. https://doi.org/10.1177/1362361316671012

Levy, S. E., Giarelli, E., Lee, L.-C., Schieve, L. A., Kirby, R. S., Cunniff, C., ... Rice, C. E. (2010). Autism Spectrum Disorder and Co-occurring Developmental, Psychiatric, and Medical Conditions Among Children in Multiple Populations of the United States: *Developmental & Behavioral Pediatrics*, 31(4), 267–275. https://doi.org/10.1097/DBP.0b013e3181d5d03b

Little, L. (2002) Middle-class mother's perceptions of peer and sibling victimisation among children with Asperger's syndrome and nonverbal learning disorders. *Issues in Comprehensive Pediatric Nursing*, 25:1, 43-57. https://doi.org/10.1080/014608602753504847

Locke, J., Ishijima, E. H., Kasari, C. and London, N. (2010). Loneliness, friendship quality and the social networks of adolescents with high-functioning autism in an inclusive school setting. *Journal of Research in Special Educational Needs*, 10, 74-81. https://doi.org/10.1111/j.1471-3802.2010.01148.x

Lombardo, M. V., Barnes, J. L., Wheelwright, S. J. & Baron-Cohen, S. (2007). Self-Referential Cognition and Empathy in Autism. *PLoS ONE 2(9): e883*. https://doi.org/10.1371/journal.pone.0000883

Lin, P.-Y., & Su, K.-P. (2007). A Meta-Analytic Review of Double-Blind, Placebo-Controlled Trials of Antidepressant

Efficacy of Omega-3 Fatty Acids. *The Journal of Clinical Psychiatry,* 68(07), 1056–1061. https://doi.org/10.4088/JCP.v68n0712

Luders, E., Toga, A. W., Lepore, N., & Gaser, C. (2009). The underlying anatomical correlates of long-term meditation: Larger hippocampal and frontal volumes of gray matter. *NeuroImage,* 45(3), 672–678

Magalhães, E. S., Pinto-Mariz, F., Bastos-Pinto, S., Pontes, A. T., Prado, E. A., & deAzevedo, L. C. (2009). Immune allergic response in Asperger syndrome. *Journal of Neuroimmunology,* 216(1–2), 108–112. https://doi.org/10.1016/j.jneuroim.2009.09.015

Mandy, W., & Tchanturia, K. (2015). Do women with eating disorders who have social and flexibility difficulties really have autism? A case series. *Molecular Autism,* 6(1), 6. https://doi.org/10.1186/2040-2392-6-6

McElhanon, B. O., McCracken, C., Karpen, S., & Sharp, W. G. (2014). Gastrointestinal Symptoms in Autism Spectrum Disorder: A Meta-analysis. *Pediatrics,* 133(5), 872–883. https://doi.org/10.1542/peds.2013-3995

Meilleur, A.-A. S., Jelenic, P., & Mottron, L. (2015). Prevalence of Clinically and Empirically Defined Talents and Strengths in Autism. *Journal of Autism and Developmental Disorders,* 45(5), 1354–1367. https://doi.org/10.1007/s10803-014-2296-2

Mordre, M., Groholt, B., Knudsen, A.K., Sponheim, E., Mykletun, A. & Myhre, A. M. (2012). *Journal of Autism and Developmental Disorders,* 42: 920. https://doi.org/

10.1007/s10803-011-1319-5

Mottron, L., Dawson, M., Soulières, I., Hubert, B., & Burack, J. (2006). Enhanced Perceptual Functioning in Autism: An Update, and Eight Principles of Autistic Perception. *Journal of Autism and Developmental Disorders*, 36(1), 27–43. https://doi.org/10.1007/s10803-005-0040-7

Neufeld, J., Roy, M., Zapf, A., Sinke, C., Emrich, H. M., Prox-Vagedes, V., ... Zedler, M. (2013). Is synesthesia more common in patients with Asperger syndrome? *Frontiers in Human Neuroscience*. https://doi.org/10.3389/fnhum.2013.00847

Ohlsson Gotby, V., Lichtenstein, P., Långström, N., & Pettersson, E. (2018). Childhood neurodevelopmental disorders and risk of coercive sexual victimization in childhood and adolescence—A population-based prospective twin study. *Journal of Child Psychology and Psychiatry*, 59(9), 957–965. https://doi.org/10.1111/jcpp.12884

Pellicano, E., & Burr, D. (2012). When the world becomes 'too real': A Bayesian explanation of autistic perception. *Trends in Cognitive Sciences*, 16(10), 504–510. https://doi.org/10.1016/j.tics.2012.08.009

Poirier, M., Martin, J. S., Gaigg, S. B., & Bowler, D. M. (2011). Short-term memory in autism spectrum disorder. *Journal of Abnormal Psychology*, 120(1), 247–252. https://doi.org/10.1037/a0022298

Quartier, A., Chatrousse, L., Redin, C., Keime, C., Haumesser, N., Maglott-Roth, A., Brino, L., Le Gras, S., Benchoua, A., Mandel., J. & Piton, A. (2018). Genes and Pathways

Regulated by Androgens in Human Neural Cells, Potential Candidates for the Male Excess in Autism Spectrum Disorder. *Biological Psychiatry Journal*, Volume 84, Issue 4, 239–252. https://doi.org/10.1016/j.biopsych.2018.01.002

Ramel, W., Goldin, P. R., Carmona, P. E., & McQuaid, J. R. (2004). The Effects of Mindfulness Meditation on Cognitive Processes and Affect in Patients with Past Depression. *Cognitive Therapy and Research*, 28(4), 433–455. https://doi.org/10.1023/B:COTR.0000045557.15923.96

Ratto, A.B., Kenworthy, L., Yerys, B.E., Bascom, J., Wieckowski, A. T., White, S. W., Wallace, G. L., Pugliese, C., Schultz, R. T., Ollendick, T. H., Scarpa, A., Seese, S., Register-Brown, K., Martin, A., & Anthony, L. G. (2018). *Journal of Autism and Developmental Disorders*, 48: 1698. https://doi.org/10.1007/s10803-017-3413-9

Remington, A., Swettenham, J., & Lavie, N. (2012). Lightening the Load: Perceptual Load Impairs Visual Detection in Typical Adults but Not in Autism. *Journal of Abnormal Psychology*, 121, 544–551. https://doi.org/10.1037/a0027670

Richa, S., Fahed, M., Khoury, E. & Mishara, B. (2014). Suicide in Autism Spectrum Disorders. *Archives of Suicide Research*, 18:4, 327-339. https://doi.org/10.1080/13811118.2013.824834

Richdale, A. L., & Schreck, K. A. (2009). Sleep problems in autism spectrum disorders: Prevalence, nature, & possible biopsychosocial aetiologies. *Sleep Medicine*

Reviews, 13(6), 403–411. https://doi.org/10.1016/j.smrv.2009.02.003

Rosa, S. D. R. (n.d.). The Problem With Autistic Communication Is Non-Autistic People: A Conversation With Dr. Catherine Crompton. Retrieved 20 August 2019, from http://www.thinkingautismguide.com/2019/05/the-problem-with-autistic-communication.html

Rotheram-Fuller, E., Kasari, C., Chamberlain, B. and Locke, J. (2010). Social involvement of children with autism spectrum disorders in elementary school classrooms. *Journal of Child Psychology and Psychiatry,* 51: 1227-1234. https://doi.org/10.1111/j.1469-7610.2010.02289.x

Rudman, L. A., & Glick, P. (2001). Prescriptive Gender Stereotypes and Backlash Toward Agentic Women. *Journal of Social Issues,* Vol. 57, No. 4, 743–762. https://doi.org/10.1111/0022-4537.00239

Russel, G., Steer, C., & Golding, J. (2010). Social and demographic factors that influence the diagnosis of autistic spectrum disorders. *Social Psychiatry and Psychiatric Epidemiology,* Volume 46: 1283, Issue 12, 1283–1293. https://doi.org/10.1007/s00127-010-0294-z

Rutherford, M., & Subiaul, F. (2016). Children with autism spectrum disorder have an exceptional explanatory drive. *Autism,* 20(6), 744–753. https://doi.org/10.1177/1362361315605973

Schuch, F. B., Vancampfort, D., Richards, J., Rosenbaum, S., Ward, P. B., & Stubbs, B. (2016). Exercise as a treatment for depression: A meta-analysis adjusting for publication bias. *Journal of Psychiatric Research, 77*, 42–51. https://doi.org/10.1016/j.jpsychires.2016.02.023

Segers, M. & Rawana, J. (2014). Systematic review of suicidality in ASD. *Autism Res, 7*, 507-521. https://doi.org/10.1002/aur.1375

Smith, H., & Milne, E. (2009, March 1). Reduced change blindness suggests enhanced attention to detail in individuals with autism. https://doi.org/10.1111/j.1469-7610.2008.01957.x

Spek, A. A., van Ham, N. C., & Nyklíček, I. (2013). Mindfulness-based therapy in adults with an autism spectrum disorder: A randomized controlled trial. *Research in Developmental Disabilities, 34*(1), 246–253. https://doi.org/10.1016/j.ridd.2012.08.009

Stanutz, S., Wapnick, J., & Burack, J. A. (2014). Pitch discrimination and melodic memory in children with autism spectrum disorders. *Autism: The International Journal of Research and Practice, 18*(2), 137–147. https://doi.org/10.1177/1362361312462905

Stewart, M. E., Barnard, L., Pearson, J., Hasan, R., & O'Brien, G. (2006). Presentation of depression in autism and Asperger syndrome: A review. *Autism, 10*(1), 103–116. https://doi.org/10.1177/1362361306062013

Tang, Y.-Y., Lu, Q., Geng, X., Stein, E. A., Yang, Y., & Posner, M. I. (2010). Short-term meditation induces white matter changes in the anterior cingulate. *Proceedings of the National Academy of Sciences, 107*(35), 15649–15652. https://doi.org/10.1073/pnas.1011043107

Thoresen, S. & Hjemdal, O. (2014). Vold og voldekt i Norge: En nasjonal forekomststudie av vold i et livsøpsperspektiv. *Nasjonalt kunnskapssenter om vold og traumatisk stress, Rapport 1/2014.* https://www.nkvts.no/content/uploads/2015/11/vold_og_voldtekt_i_norge.pdf

Walker, M. (2017). *Why We Sleep [kindle format]* (1st edition). Penguin.

Ward, J., Hoadley, C., Hughes, J. E. A., Smith, P., Allison, C., Baron-Cohen, S., & Simner, J. (2017). Atypical sensory sensitivity as a shared feature between synaesthesia and autism. *Scientific Reports, 7,* 41155

Weeks, Boshoff, & Stewart. (2012). Systematic review of the effectiveness of the Wilbarger protocol with children. *Pediatric Health, Medicine and Therapeutics, 79.* https://doi.org/10.2147/phmt.S37173

Weiss, J. A., & Fardella, M. A. (2018). Victimization and Perpetration Experiences of Adults With Autism. *Frontiers in Psychiatry, 9.* https://doi.org/10.3389/fpsyt.2018.00203

Willey, L. (2014). *Pretending to be Normal: Living with Asperger's Syndrome (Autism Spectrum Disorder) [kindle format]* (Expanded ed). Retrieved from https://www.amazon.co.uk/gp/product/B00N18C0OW/ref=kinw_myk_ro_title

Zahid, S. & Upthegrove, R. (2017). Suicidality in Autistic Spectrum Disorders A Systematic Review. *Crisis,* 38(4), 237–246. https://doi.org/10.1027/0227-5910/a000458

Zwaigenbaum, L., Bryson, S.E., Szatmari, P. Brian, J., Smith, I.

M., Roberts, W., Vallaincourt, T. & Roncadin, C. (2012). *Journal of Autism and Developmental Disorders,* 42: 2585. https://doi.org/10.1007/s10803-012-1515-y

Printed in Great Britain
by Amazon